Fennec Fox

Fennec Fox Owner's Manual

Fennec Fox care, costs, pros and cons, training, health and feeding.

by

Edward Eldington

Published by: IMB Publishing

Table of Contents

Chapter 1: Introduction

The Fennec Fox (*Fennecus zerda*, previously *Vulpes zerda* and a member of the genus Vulpus) is the smallest fox in the world. It has been part of the exotic pet market for many years. However, after it was introduced – in all its cuteness – to the world in the animated Disney film *Zootopia,* the demand for these tiny canids has greatly increased.

These foxes are native to North Africa and Asia. Their range stretches from Morocco to Egypt, south to Niger and east to Kuwait and the Sinai Peninsula. Specifically, these little foxes are found in Egypt, Chad, Morocco, Niger, Mali, Libya, Sudan, Northern Sinai, Tunisia, the Western Sahara and Algeria where it is the national animal.

Their natural habitat is deserts or very arid regions. They dig their dens in sand dunes or in open areas where there are plants that provide some shelter. Stable sand dunes close to some vegetation are their first choice and they tend to create burrows near the base of the dunes where the moisture levels are higher. Dens are lined with plant matter that can be used as food or a source of liquid when needed.

Fennecs are social creatures and live in communities of at least 10 individuals. Dens are often interconnected and tunnels may be as long as 34 feet or approximately 10 meters. The dens themselves are usually several feet below the surface.

These foxes got their name from the Arabic word *fanak,* which means "fox". The species name, *zerda,* is derived from the Greek word for dry and refers to the desert habitat of these little creatures.

On the topic of names, a male fox is known as a reynard, females as vixens and a baby fox is known as a kit. A group is called a leash or a skulk of foxes.

This book will introduce you to these beautiful small foxes by discussing their appearance and biology, typical behavior, their environment and feeding requirements, their personalities and what makes them good – and not-so-good – pets.

In other words, this book aims to tell you what you need to know so you can decide whether or not this is the exotic pet for you and, if it is, how to select your Fennec Fox, what you need to buy before you bring it home, and how to take proper care of it.

All the necessary equipment, food and the general environment that has a crucial bearing on the health and happiness of Fennec Foxes will also be discussed.

The Fennec Fox is a hardy creature. However, they can become ill and anyone who is serious about having an exotic pet needs to know what to look for and how to deal with common ailments.

I hope that you find this book both useful and fun to read!

Chapter 2: Fennec Fox basics

1) Fennec Fox overview

The Fennec Fox (*Fennecus zerda*) is also known as the Desert Fox, the Sun Fox – due to the fact that they enjoy basking and sleeping in the sun – and simply the fennec. These nocturnal mammals are the smallest of all the fox species and also of the *canid* family, which consists of foxes, wolves, jackals, coyotes, and the domestic dog.

There has been some disagreement over whether fennecs are true foxes and part of the genus *Vulpus,* which includes other fox types, or whether they in fact belong to a separate genus. This is due to the fact that although the fennec is similar to other foxes, there are also several significant differences in terms of both physical and behavioral characteristics.

These differences are that fennecs live in packs while most fox species are solitary. Fennecs also have a lower chromosome count: 32 pairs as opposed to the 35 to 39 pairs that other foxes have. Finally, the fennec does not have musk glands whereas other foxes do (this is a definite advantage in a pet fox, as musk glands produce rather overwhelming odors!).

A characteristic that makes the Fennec Fox so easy to identify is without doubt its extraordinarily large ears. Their bat-like ears grow to 10 to 15 centimeters or 4 to 6 inches in length. This may not sound like much but in relation to the length of their bodies, which are only 24 to 41 centimeters or 9.5 to 16 inches long, they are proportionately very large ears.

Fennec Foxes are opportunistic feeders. They forage for plants and eggs and also hunt rodents, reptiles, and insects. About 90% of their diet consists of proteins.

These foxes can jump up to 2 feet or 61 centimeters high and leap about 4 feet or 120 centimeters to pounce on prey. Their very sensitive ears can hear prey moving underground and this combined with their talent for digging makes them very effective hunters. What's more, these little foxes can run at high speeds and change direction very quickly.

As is the case with most animals that live in deserts, fennecs can go a long time without water. They have evolved to obtain the water they need from what they eat and to restrict water loss to a remarkable degree.

Fennec foxes are usually found living in family groups of ten individuals. Pairs mate for life. They are highly social animals and enjoy playing and spending time together. They also make a wide range of sounds to communicate with each other.

2) Life span or expectancy

In the wild the Fennec Fox has a life expectancy of up to 10 years. However, these foxes have not been well studied in the wild. If they are well cared for in captivity they can reach the ripe age of 14.

3) Enemies and predators

These foxes do have enemies. The main one is, not surprisingly, the human being. While fennecs are not eaten in countries such as Morocco, as the meat is considered 'dirty', they do enter the meat market in other areas and countries. They are primarily captured for the pet trade and for their attractive, thick fur. Young fennecs are sold at the sides of the road or in towns to tourists.

The other significant predators are the various varieties of African eagle owl and domestic dogs. Scientific rather than anecdotal evidence of predation by carnivores such as hyenas, jackals and caracals has yet to be found.

In more general terms, the spread of human settlements and activities is increasing in areas where these foxes are found. With this comes an expanding transport network and the vehicles on them pose a risk to any fox crossing a road or railway line.

4) Fennec Fox appearance and biology

Size and weight:

The fennec is the smallest canid in the world. Adults only reach 8 inches or 20 centimeters in height (at the shoulder) and weigh between 1 and 1.5 kilograms or 2.2 to 3.3 pounds. Male fennecs are slightly larger than females.

The body reaches 9 to 16 inches (23 to 40.5 centimeters) in length and the tail grows to a length of 7 to 12 inches (18 to 30.5 centimeters). The only large thing about the Fennec fox is its ears: 4 to 6 inches (10 to 15 centimeters)!

In comparative terms, a fully-grown fennec is approximately the same size as an adult Chihuahua dog.

Color and markings:

The fur of the fennec serves to keep them warm during the very cold desert nights, reflect the sun and help to keep them cooler during the fiercely hot days and provide camouflage to protect them from predators.

Their coats are thick and soft and predominantly a cream or light beige in color. It is this sandy coloring that helps them to blend into their surroundings. The underbelly, however, is white.

The fur on their faces is lighter than on their bodies. They have a darker streak that runs downwards from the inner eye to either side of the muzzle.

Their splendid, furry tails (sometimes called a "sweep") have black tips and a dark patch of bristles at the base of the tail covering the anal gland. Not only do their tails help them to change direction very rapidly, but also foxes curl up to sleep and their tails keep their feet and noses warm.

Their legs are slender. Foxes living in North Africa are slightly reddish. Fennecs that live further south have much paler, even white legs.

Other interesting fennec facts:

➢ These little foxes have large black eyes, which are ideally structured and evolved for their nocturnal hunting.

➢ Greatly thanks to their oversized ears, they have extremely acute hearing. This allows them to hear prey at great distances and even underground.

➢ Their teeth are like those of domestic dogs and other canids.

➢ When truly content and relaxed, these small foxes make sounds similar to the purr produced by cats.

Special desert adaptations:

The fennec has evolved to be perfectly suited to life in a very harsh environment. From behavioral adaptations such as sleeping in cool, deep burrows in the heat of the day and hunting at night to biological features these little creatures are amazing desert dwellers.

There are several primary ways in which fennec biology deals with life in very hot and water-poor surroundings:

1. *Ears*: these extraordinarily large ears are rich in blood vessels, which lie close to the surface of the skin. This allows the fennec to dissipate heat into the atmosphere. Heat radiates from their large ears and this helps to keep them cool on even the hottest days.

2. *Coat*: Their coats are very effective at reflecting the suns rays, which helps fennecs to stay cooler than they otherwise would.

3. *Kidneys*: The Fennec Fox is able to live without abundant water. In other words, it doesn't need to drink water in order to survive. They appear to obtain all the moisture and hydration they need from the plant matter they eat. In addition, their kidneys have developed in such a way as to restrict water loss.

4. *Metabolism:* The metabolic rate of fennecs is only two thirds that of other animals of the same size. In addition, their resting heartbeat of 118 beats per minute is 40% lower than other

similarly sized animals. Both of these help these foxes to stay cool and conserve moisture.

5. *Body temperature*: Fennecs can regulate and control their body temperature to a quite remarkable degree. A fennec's normal body temperature is 100.8° Fahrenheit or 38.2° Celsius.

    They will only start to shiver in order to raise their body temperature if ambient temperatures drop to 68° Fahrenheit / 20° Celsius.

    When temperatures rise, a fennec will only begin to pant when the temperature reaches 95° Fahrenheit or 35° Celsius or above. A full pant is reserved for heat in excess of 100° Fahrenheit or 38° Celsius. Importantly, the fennec's tongue is kept curled inside the mouth when it pants and this reduces saliva/liquid loss significantly.

    Sweating doesn't take place until the fox's body temperature reaches a scorching 105.6° Fahrenheit or 40.9° Celsius. If the fox can stay in its burrow in the heat of the day, or the shade of vegetation or rocks, it is unlikely to reach this temperature and start to lose precious fluid.

5) The history of the Fennec Fox as a pet

The Fennec Fox has been part of the exotic pet market since the 1970's but it is not a common pet. However, this may change.

Their popularity appears to be increasing thanks to the 2016 Disney Studios film titled *Zootopia*. The animated film features a fennec called Finnick. Despite the fact that the character is not all that endearing, the tiny fox with its huge ears has captured the heart and imagination of audiences.

Although fennecs are still captured in the wild for the pet trade, there are now commercial breeding programs too. The young foxes or kits are removed from their mother before they have been weaned so that they can be bottle-fed and hand reared.

It is believed that doing this results in a tamer and better-socialized fox. While these traits are certainly desirable, it does mean that commercially bred fennecs are more expensive. It should also be kept in mind that even these fennecs can't accurately be described as domesticated; they are still wild animals.

The breeding, registration and classification of fennecs as a pet is more advanced in the United States than elsewhere. The Department of Agriculture describes the fennec as a "small wild/exotic canid" and the fennec and the silver fox are the only fox species that may be kept as a pet in America. The US has also established a registry for breeders in an effort to monitor the program and guard against inbreeding.

Another reason why the fennec's popularity as a pet remains fairly modest is that they are not easy to train… They are often affectionate towards their people and dogs in particular, are always delightfully energetic critters and lovely to look at.

6) Social behavior

In the wild Fennec Foxes live in closely knit family groups of about ten individuals. This group includes the primary and monogamous breeding pair. The males mark and defend their territory with urine, especially during mating season. They can become extremely aggressive with other males who are being threatening or encroaching on their turf.

All fennecs are athletic and playful and they enjoy a rough and tumble or a game with each other. One should keep in mind, though, that they spend a staggering 65% of their time asleep! When they are awake they are irrepressible and demand attention and things to do.

Hand-reared fennecs are far more likely to be loving and affectionate with an owner, but wild-caught foxes may calm down with time and careful handling. It is important to keep in mind that both wild caught and bottle-fed fennecs are *not* domestic animals; they are still wild. They can also be rather reclusive, shy and skittish.

When approached a fennec may cower or lie down on its side and wag its tail while yelping. If they feel more comfortable, happy and unthreatened a fennec may purr like a cat.

A word to the wise: fennecs are small, *very* fast and *very* quite. This means that it's easy to step on them or kick them by mistake, which will lead to terrible injuries. Many owners have found that putting a collar with a bell on it around a fennec's neck helps to warn one when they are around and moving.

Given that fennecs are very active and need high energy play time, they are better suited to an environment where they have a space they can safely dash about in and an owner who can spend a meaningful amount of time with them.

If an owner doesn't spend enough time bonding with a fennec and socializing it when it is young, it can lead to behavioral problems later. Owners may even feel the desire to rehome an adult fennec because it is a "handful". This is grossly unfair to the fennec and whoever takes it on.

7) Myths & misunderstandings about Fennec Foxes

The Fennec Fox is endangered

No, they aren't. Admittedly, there has been very limited observation of this species and figures are based on observations by those who trap fennecs for the pet and fur trades and people living in areas where fennecs naturally occur.

There is enough information for the International Union for the Conservation of Nature (IUCN) to class the fennec as "Least Concern" on their Red List. This means that while the species is not thought to be threatened, the trade in these foxes should be controlled.

For this reason, fennecs are an Appendix II animal in terms of the Convention on International Trade in Endangered Species (CITES). In other words, the cross-border movement or travel of the fennec is restricted and controlled.

As a result, fennecs are illegal in some places and not in others. Anyone wanting to obtain a fennec should check country, state, and city bylaws and ordinances first. If a fennec is owned illegally the authorities will confiscate it. This is not what the pet owner wants but is even worse for the fennec, which will be euthanized.

Fennecs are omnivores

This is a popular myth and came about because in the wild fennecs do eat some plant matter. However, this is not because they are omnivores but because it is how this species obtains water in arid, desert environments.

Fennecs are in fact obligate carnivores like domestic cats that also eat small amounts of plant matter from time to time but need a diet full of taurine-rich meat (more on diet later).

Omnivores have grinding molars at the back of their mouths that allow them to properly chew plants and vegetation. Fennecs, like all canids (the fox family) don't have these kinds of teeth. They are not designed to cope with a predominantly plant-based diet.

Fennecs have weak teeth but they are ideally suited to the diet of a fennec in the wild: soft, sometimes slightly crunchy, insects.

Fennecs smell

This is also not true and the reason is fairly straightforward: fennecs, unlike other fox species, don't have musk glands. This means they don't have a strong odor. The second factor that means that they are not smelly is the fact that, like cats, they are clean by nature and spend a fair amount of time grooming. However, their fecal matter is unpleasant…

It's legal everywhere to have fennecs as pets

As previously mentioned, Fennec Foxes are not legal everywhere.

For those living in the US things are especially complex, with variation from state to state, city to city and county to county. It's essential to see where fennecs are permitted and where not. In some places in America fennec owners must have a United States Department of Agriculture (USDA) license.

In the UK things are a lot easier: it is legal to own a fennec and no license is needed. Neighbors should be consulted, though, in case they don't like the idea.

Chapter 3: The Fennec Fox as a pet

1) Overview

Depending on who you ask, fennecs are described as being like dogs, cats or even ferrets in temperament and personality. Some say that these little foxes are a happy combination of dog and cat characteristics. Of course, comparing a fennec to a domesticated animal is not a fair comparison.

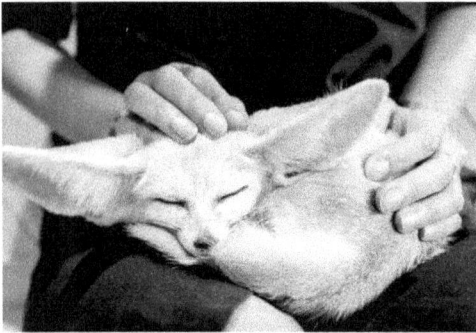

The cat analogy stems from the fact that they sleep a lot, are very agile and can jump to great heights, can be a little aloof, are independent and when they want a cuddle they want it now! Fennecs are about the size of a large, adult cat.

Their energy, playfulness and social nature with other canids are more dog-like characteristics.

The ferret comparison is thanks to their curiosity, tendency to climb into, onto or behind anything and the very high levels of energy both animals exhibit. One owner described fennecs as being like ferrets on hyper-drive.

Be warned, though. Fennecs need careful socialization and to be kept safe, as they are escape artists. Because they have boundless energy it needs to be channeled; having a toilet roll shredded is nothing compared to having your couch or mattress turned into a burrow. They need entertainment and exercise.

Generally speaking, a fennec sleeps 65% of its time, 20% just relaxing (preferably in the sun) and the remaining 15% in a state of high, constant activity. If they have no animal companion you need to provide all the stimulation and play!

Fennecs are likely to get on well with dogs. However, some canids want to be 'top-dog' and this can cause friction. Socializing and training can help to prevent or alleviate this problem.

2) Fennecs and other pets

There are some basic facts and simple guidelines when it comes to fennecs and other pets:

- Use common sense when bringing a new pet into the household. Introduce the newcomer slowly and in a strictly controlled environment.

- Fennecs do better with dogs (fellow canids, after all) than they do with cats. In fact, if an owner doesn't invest time with their fennec, especially when it is young or has first arrived, and maintain the socializing process, the fennec will bond better with a dog than with a person.

- It's wise to limit a young or newly arrived fennec's time with other animals so the bond with the owner is strengthened and the bond with another animal does not become the primary one.

- Fennecs should not ever be left alone with a domestic animal as they can be unpredictable and have been known to turn on pets, especially cats.

- A large dog might accidentally injure a fennec during the course of a game, as fennec's bones break quite easily. Games should therefore be supervised.

- If a pet is the right size to fit in a fennec's mouth, keep them apart! A small pet rodent or a bird *will* become fennec food… The rule is that a pet will be safe it is the same size or larger than the fennec.

- A fennec is in all probability far bouncier for far longer than the average cat or dog can or wants to be. The fennec will want to play and will try to even if the dog or cat does *not* share the desire. This may lead to some friction.

3) Fennecs and children

Children who are 7 and older need to be shown how to handle and deal with a fennec. Even if they have been taught what to do and not to do, their time together should be supervised. On the other hand, children who are younger than 7 are not a good combination with these little foxes. Fennecs have a tendency to nip and, like all animals, may even bite if they are hurt or feel frightened. Small children are more likely to be injured, as their skin is still sensitive and thinner than that of older children and adults.

Most small children will find it hard to understand why this pet needs to be treated differently. A little child might even hurt or scare a fennec unintentionally by handling it in a rough or clumsy way.

4) Fennecs and strangers in your home

Fennecs are like all creatures: some are more outgoing and gregarious than others. As a result, some fennecs may enjoy being around new people and others will be frightened. Fennecs are a little unpredictable and skittish… On balance the odds are that a fennec will not be thrilled to meet new people. Keep in mind that fennecs, like other fox species, communicate in part though nips, nibbles and the occasional bite. Your visitors may not appreciate this!

If one wants a fennec to be more sociable it gets back to the fact that an owner must put a lot of time and effort into socializing a fennec when it is young; it's too late when the fox is older.

5) The fennec's personality

A fennec, regardless of age, is a combination of snuggly and hyperactive… when it's not fast asleep.

A correctly socialized fennec will enjoy playing, cuddling and being pet. They also like curling up on a welcoming lap for a nap or a sleep and a boisterous game will rarely be refused.

When socialized well, fennecs are able to differentiate between one person and another and will bond more closely with the individual who spends the most time with them.

Like domestic dogs and horses, fennecs groom themselves and each other by gently nibbling through their fur. This behavior also establishes and strengthens social bonds. If, while petting your fennec, you find your fingers or knuckles being gently (and sometimes a little painfully) nibbled you can celebrate, as it is a sign of acceptance!

As with dogs and – to an even greater degree – cats, you need to learn to understand a fennec's body language and the sounds it makes. For example, is your fennec wriggling with delight at being held and having its tummy rubbed or because it has had enough and wants to get away? The first is happiness for both of you. The second could mean a nip for you and distress for your fennec. This understanding and knowledge comes with time, as each fennec is unique.

In addition to sweet, affectionate (once socialized), agile and full of high-speed energy, fennecs are also really smart. However, this doesn't mean they are easy to train!

Chapter 4: The downside of fennecs as pets

These beautiful, small foxes do make endearing and most unusual pets. However, before buying one you need to know that there are things that can be unexpected or hard to handle.

1) General

Fennecs are not suitable if you live in a flat or apartment or any kind of rented accommodation. They need space, they need time outdoors and they can be noisy. Fennecs can also do damage, which a landlord won't, understandably, take kindly to. If you rent property you could find yourself asked to leave!

2) Fennecs are escape artists

Between their agility, energy, climbing abilities, strength, speed and digging prowess these foxes are excellent escape artists. Their high levels of activity and curiosity also add to the chance that a fennec will escape unless it is properly housed (more on this later), supervised and socialized.

This can't be said enough: fennecs are *not* domesticated animals. At worst they are wild animals and at best, when socialized, they are tame wild animals.

If you take a fennec out for a walk and it gets scared or spots a potential meal it will wriggle out of an ordinary collar or badly fitting harness and be off like a shot, probably never to be seen again.

3) Fennecs need a lot of attention

Because fennecs are wild animals, to tame them requires a great deal of time and attention. If you travel a lot or have a number of things that take up your time and attention a fennec is not for you.

If you have been away for some time your fennec may not even know who you are when you get back. In addition, without adequate time and attention from you, even a tame fennec may revert to being wild. Some owners say that a fennec shouldn't even be left overnight during the first year.

These foxes need far more socializing than dogs and cats and more play and bonding time too so that they stay interested in their owners and people in general.

You will have to spend time playing with a fennec, feeding it, cleaning its pen or enclosure, and maintaining socialization.

4) Fennecs can get underfoot

These little foxes are very fast and are in almost constant motion when awake and extremely quite. Like some domestic pets they have a tendency to run between one's feet.

As a fennec owner you need to be aware all the time of where your fox is so it doesn't get trodden on or kicked. While doing the same to a dog or cat will be very painful for it, a similar injury to a fennec is likely to result in broken bones.

5) Fennecs are prone to nipping

Fennecs nibble to be affectionate and bond but they nip or even bite when frightened, hurt or "cage aggressive"/inadequately socialized.

As a general rule, females are less hyperactive but more prone to nipping than males. Male foxes that have not been neutered are of course far more nippy and aggressive during mating season.

Owners have also been nipped when trying to take something away from their fennec. A good strategy to avoid this is to trade: offer the fox a replacement item.

6) Nasty and/or tricky habits fennecs have…

There's no getting around the fact that there are several less savory aspects of fennec behavior you have to prevent – or just plain accept – if you have one of these little canids. These include:

- They love to dig and they are very good at it. This has implications for floors, furniture, mattresses, doors, walls and any other surface or object a fennec might decide to dig into (or least try very hard to burrow into or through) and damage.

- They are cunning little thieves and will steal and hide things, from shiny objects that catch their eye, items of clothing to the Sunday roast and other food items.

- They are fond of grabbing and chewing metal, leather and rubber objects. These could include items of jewelry, car keys, coins, rubber bands, elastic, gloves or foil. These objects and materials pose a choking and other health hazards and are not what you want a fennec to chew or swallow.

- Fennecs are not at all easy to train so training them is slow, time consuming and carries only a small chance and certainly no guarantee of success.

- Because they are active, energetic, curious, agile and like to burrow they can leave a mess and total chaos in their wake.

- Although they keep themselves clean, they're not bothered about where they relieve themselves. They may even mess in their bedding and 'accidents' are more likely when a fennec is excited. As one owner said, "if you cannot tolerate poop in inappropriate places then a fennec is not for you".

- Fennecs spray, even if neutered or spayed, to mark their territory.

The good news is that many of these drawbacks can be avoided by (a) having an enclosure for your fennec, (b) making and keeping your home 'fennec-proof' and (c) supervising your fox when he or she is not in their cage or enclosure.

7) Fennecs are vocal

Female fennecs are usually a little quieter than their male counterparts but the bottom line is that fennecs are noisy. The sounds they make when they are happy or excited, such as when they are playing a game, can be very loud and high-pitched.

In addition to their excited playtime screams, fennecs produce a number of other sounds: squeaks, growls, yips, purrs, bird-like trills, barks and howling or wailing. They are particularly loud at night. Even if this doesn't bother the owner, neighbors may object!

As with all other animals, some are far noisier than others; some fennecs are fairly quiet and only vocal when greeting their owner.

8) Fennecs and odor

As previously stated, thanks to their lack of musk glands fennecs have virtually no body odor.

The exception is when they are very frightened and release a scent from the glands under their tails. However, it is not overwhelming and only lasts a minute or two.

Unfortunately, the same cannot be said for the urine and feces, which are very pungent. One can overcome this by keeping the cage and area they are in clear of waste matter.

9) X-rated fennec behavior

There's no polite way to say this: fennecs are, like some species of dogs, rather oversexed creatures. They make amorous advances towards anything: objects, legs, other pets and anything else that's handy.

This is not ideal at the best of times but it is especially awkward and embarrassing when it happens in front of children or visitors.

Some fennec owners have had some luck with encouraging their fennec to restrict its activities to a stuffed toy that is dedicated to the purpose.

Chapter 5: Buying your Fennec Fox

So you still like the idea of having a Fennec Fox as a pet? Well done! Now it's time to look at choosing the right fox for you.

1) How old should a Fennec Fox be?

While it may seem that getting a very young fennec would help with bonding and socializing, that is not in fact the case. With these little foxes, there is an ideal period or window in terms of the best age to get one. There is no denying that babies, regardless of species, are cute and very hard to resist.

The same is certainly true of baby fennecs. But you need to try. The primary reason for this is that these little foxes are very hard to bottle feed. This is thanks to the fact that they are prone to drinking very fast and aspirate as a result.

Ideally you should get a fennec youngster that has been weaned and is therefore 8 to 10 weeks old. There are quite a few breeders that will actually not release fennecs before they have been successfully weaned.

On the other hand, a fennec that is older than 3 or 4 months is also not a good bet. A fox that is older than this will be harder to socialize and bond with and training will be even tougher than usual.

2) Selecting a Fennec Fox breeder

In the US it's easier than in other countries to locate a breeder because of the registry and other official measures. In the States, a professional breeder should be able to provide his or her USDA license number to a potential buyer. If he or she does not have a license, think hard before buying a fennec from the breeder.

Be suspicious of 'cheap' fennecs advertised for rehoming. In all likelihood the owners want to get rid of them because of health or behavioral issues. You don't need to inherit them!

At time of writing there is no such regulation in the UK. Try to find a breeder through exotic pet websites, online Fennec Fox forums or a vet that deals with exotic pets.

3) Shipping a Fennec Fox

No animal handles shipping well. This is especially true of wild or undomesticated animals, which become extremely stressed. For this reason it's always far better to locate a local breeder. The reality is that, for most people, there is no local breeder.

If you have to have your fennec shipped to you it's a good idea to find out what measures the breeder will take to minimize shipping stress and the most direct route to use to reduce transit time as much as possible.

In addition, make sure your fennec is insured and that you keep records of all correspondence and transactions. If something were to happen the distress of losing your fennec, or it becoming ill or injured, will not be eased by your financial loses!

4) Is a male or a female better?

The answer to this question varies depending on whom you ask. As a general rule of thumb, females, whether spayed or not, are a little more nippy and skittish and are very fast moving. However, they are less vocal and a bit less hyperactive.

Males, on the other hand, tend to be more inclined to cuddle and are a little more docile *if* they are neutered. If they are not neutered they can be territorial, even aggressively so, and mark their turf with rather pungent urine.

5) One or two or more?

In the wild fennecs live in groups and they are social creatures. However, it is not essential to have more than one fennec. Of course a fennec may be happier with a companion to play and nap with. Watching two fennecs romping around is a most enjoyable experience for the owner too.

The other deciding factor for many fennec owners is expense. As can be seen in a later chapter, the purchase of and care for a fennec comes at a significant cost.

Chapter 6: What you need to buy & do for your Fennec Fox

1) Essential basic equipment & supplies

While this is not an exhaustive list, it does give an indication of the really basic items or supplies you need before you bring your Fennec Fox home:

- *Suitable food*: more on this later
- *Toys*: they may or may not play with them but toys for cats often work well, especially ones that can be chased and pounced on. No toy should be so small that it poses a choking hazard; fennecs chew things
- *Bedding*: it's advisable to have more than one piece or set, as it will need to be washed fairly regularly, especially with less successfully house-trained fennecs who will mess in their beds
- *An H-harness*: a cat-sized or small dog harness would be best, as it must fit snugly so the fennec can't wriggle or twist out of it
- *A leash*: a strong dog leash in addition to the harness is advised, as a fennec will be more secure this way
- *Litter box*: a hood or hooded litter box may be a good investment, as a fennec will dig very enthusiastically and without a hood the gravel or sand will get everywhere
- *Litter*: don't buy litter that is fine or has a tendency to clump, as it will get between a fennec's pads and toes and it will be ingested when they groom themselves
- *Puppy pads*: it can be easier to get a fennec house or toilet trained with a puppy pad than a litter box
- *Scratcher*: a scratching pad, especially a cardboard one, may help to save furniture and floors from sharp fennec claws.
- *Pet carrier*: you need a sturdy carrier that you can use when you need to take your fennec to see the vet or somewhere away from your home. A carrier designed for a small dog would be ideal in size. It must be strong so that your expert digger and wriggler can't escape.

Investing in a book or two about Fennec Foxes is also strongly recommended. The more you know about your fox and what they need the better. It also makes life much easier for an owner if he or she has all the information necessary.

If you will be setting up a larger enclosure or your fennec will have a room to itself, you will need additional items such as wooden logs, stones, a digging pit or sand box and bedding of some kind.

2) The cage or enclosure

Fennec Foxes have very specific needs when it comes to their environment. This is for their sake and that of the owner.

Simply allowing a fennec the run of the house is not an option, unless they are supervised constantly. It's also too easy for these lightning-fast mammals to escape through a window or door. They also need a 'house' that they can sleep or hide away in when they feel anxious.

Opinion is divided on what constitutes an adequately sized and interesting cage or enclosure for a fennec. What is agreed upon, though, is that these little foxes must be in an area with good ventilation, low humidity levels and their space must be fennec-proof and safe.

Some fennec owners use large ferret cages, as they have several levels and ramps. Keep in mind that the distance from one level to the next should be short, as fennecs have been known to break limbs jumping down. The largest version of a ferret cage is perhaps best for these very active and agile creatures.

These cages work well to house fennecs when they are not being supervised. However, they can't spend all their time in a cage as it is too restricting – fennecs need to be able to run – and it also provides inadequate stimulation and interest generally.

Owners must also remember that these foxes are desert dwellers so they need to be kept warm. Of course they shouldn't become overheated either. Hand-reared fennecs don't adjust to changes in temperature the way their totally wild counterparts can.

All fennecs love to lie in the sun. Ideally your fennec should have access to a sunny spot or area in which he or she can doze and just relax.

If you have a property where you can build an outdoor enclosure or a pen for your fennec, there are precautions you need to take in light of their agility and climbing and digging skills. They also need protection from the weather and potential predators such as dogs, wild foxes and large birds of prey.

Guidelines for an outdoor enclosure:

➤ The gaps in the fencing and wiring should not be large enough to allow a fennec to get a limb or head stuck in it or to wriggle through it.

Given an adult fennec's skull is 1.7 to 1.9 inches (4.3 to 4.8 centimeters) wide by 1.4 to 1.5 inches (3.55 to 3.8 centimeters) high, any gap or hole larger than the minimums will allow one of these cunning critters to get out and away. A kit's head is of course much smaller.

➤ Preferably, the enclosure should be roofed over to keep out rain and predators such as large birds and to prevent the fennec from climbing out. A roofing substance that provides protection but allows sunlight in is optimal.

➤ The floor must either be one that can't be dug through or the side fencing must be down to a depth that prevents escape through a tunnel. Keep in mind fennecs are expert and very fast diggers.

This will also help to keep domestic dogs and any other predators from getting into the enclosure.

A fence that runs down 8 to 10 feet (2.4 to 3 meters) below the surface will prevent tunnel escapes and allow fennecs to indulge in their passion for digging.

➤ In addition to their love for digging, fennecs enjoy and need to run. If you don't have space to build a wide enclosure or place several ferret cages side by side, think about building or investing in a running wheel of a diameter of 30 inches or 76 centimeters. Wheels are often only successful if a kit is introduced to one early on.

- ➤ In terms of items in a cage or enclosure, fennecs require a bed of some kind. Many enjoy bedding they can arrange and snuggle into and others even like pet-sized hammocks or the kind of pet bed that has a cover or hood.

- ➤ Some plant material that does not produce dust or pollen is a good addition.

- ➤ In large enclosures low tree stumps or smallish pieces of wood are fun for climbing onto and over or sunning themselves on.

While these large cages or enclosures are lovely for the fennec, it shouldn't spend all its time in it. Time with its owner is necessary in order to bond and become and remain socialized.

3) Fennec-proofing your home

Your house needs to be fennec proof before you bring your new pet home… and it must be kept that way for as long as you have one of these foxes. Why? The answer is because they run, jump, steal, dig, often chew and will escape if they get half a chance. And they will be like that all their lives.

In a fennec-proof home:

- ✓ The electrical outlets are covered so little paws can't investigate them

- ✓ Electrical cords are not left lying on floors because they will be chewed with potentially lethal effects

- ✓ There are no plastic bags or loose chords or wires a fennec could get tangled in

- ✓ There are no breakable items on tables or low shelves where a bouncing, running and climbing fennec can knock them off

- ✓ There are no small, loose items at a level where they can be found by a curious fox, chewed or swallowed. Keep in mind that fennecs can climb and jump up to 4 feet (1.2 meters)

✓ The toilet seats and lids are kept down to prevent drowning and injury

✓ Doors to out-of-bounds areas and the outside world are kept closed. Insect or fly screens are not adequate, as a fox can scratch through them

✓ There aren't any pot plants because they will in all likelihood be dug up.

You need to use common sense in order to safeguard your fennec *and* the things in your home that you want to protect.

Chapter 7: Introducing your Fennec Fox into its new home

1) Socializing your Fennec Fox

Socializing domesticated pets is important; it is even more vital with wild pets like fennecs. With animals, the process of socialization involves teaching them how to be around people and other pets and how to interact with them. Your fennec also needs to learn how to deal with and adjust to a range of different experiences.

The aim of socialization is to have a fox that interacts well and happily with people and other pets. The secret to this is doing all you can do ensure that your fennec only has positive associations with other animals, humans and situations within its environment.

The golden rule is to start interacting with and socializing your fennec as soon as possible. The younger the fox, the better. If a pet fox gets used to being handled and bonds with its owner it makes everything else easier. For example, training will be less onerous and visits to the vet will be less traumatic for all concerned if a fennec has become used to people and being picked up and handled.

A young fennec should be picked up frequently and then put down again. Don't try to hold him or her for too long initially. A fennec also won't respond well to having a game interrupted. It can also be helpful to reward a young fennec with a treat of some kind when you pick it up.

A good time to pick up a young fennec for a lap cuddle is when he or she is sleepy after a play session. Most fennecs reportedly enjoy having their ears, heads and the back of the necks stroked. Some also like tummy rubs and will roll onto their backs to invite one.

As with any other pet you need to get to know what your fennec does and doesn't enjoy; it will let you know if it is not enjoying something by getting off your lap or giving you a warning nip.

2) Cage training

Fennec Fox owners and breeders all seem to agree that the first item on the training agenda and an important part of getting a fennec settled into its new home is cage training. In addition to helping your fox settle, cage training also helps to avoid or greatly reduce cage aggression.

However, you need to have established a bond with your fennec before tackling any training including cage training.

The purpose of this type of training is to get a fennec to go into its cage so that it's not an unhappy battle for both of you when your fennec needs to be secured in its cage. It's crucial, though, that a fennec learns to associate its cage with comfort and safety and *not* with punishment or being trapped.

You don't want to force him or her in. Ideally a fennec should discover the cage and enter it on its own. The best ways to achieve this include using enticements to lure your fox inside. Foxes are smart so you need to:

➢ Use really special treats as 'bait'. For example, large worms or crickets are popular.

➢ Don't use the same food each time.

➢ Instead of always using food, use a toy as enticement sometimes instead. For instance, throw a toy your fennec likes to play with into the cage so it follows it in.

Because the cage should not be associated with anything negative, don't always lock it. Only do so when you are going out or to bed and you have to lock it.

Chapter 8: Training your pet fennec

1) A note on training generally

There are two things to remember when you are training a fennec: be very, very patient and be prepared for the fact that it may not work.

These foxes are notoriously hard to train although a few owners report success with a range of training and activities. They are, after all, wild animals and don't share a domestic dog's desire to please their owner. Fennecs, like some cats, please themselves only!

In other words, a fennec will do something if there is something in it for them. There is no guarantee, however, that it will repeat the activity next time!

In order to try to train a fennec, you should build on or use things a fennec knows instinctively or has learnt because it suits it such as chasing a moving object or the sound of the fridge or a treat packet opening. Again as with cats, clicker training can be effective with fennecs.

As with any type of training with all kinds of animals, the earlier you make a start the better. Sessions should also be kept short as these active, hyper little foxes have short attention spans. Training sessions should be frequent to reinforce behavior, however.

2) Clicker training

It is suggested that you should arm yourself with the following items: a training clicker (which can be purchased at any good pet shop or online store), treats that your fennec will find irresistible and a stick such as a dowel rod painted a bright color at one end.

Step 1: Show the clicker to your fennec and allow him or her to sniff it (not chew it) so it knows it's not scary.

Step 2: Click it once and immediately give your fennec a treat. Do this 5 times in each training session so that the connection between the clicker's sound and a treat is made. It is suggested that one should hold 3 or 4 clicker training sessions a day.

Important note: don't ever use the clicker when you are not training or not wanting to elicit a trained behavior because your fennec will become confused and the training will be less effective.

Step 3: When your fennec is comfortable with the clicker, move onto using the target (the stick with the colored tip). Hold the stick out but be careful not to make any sudden movements that your fennec might find frightening or threatening and wait for it to touch the end of the stick with its nose. It will do this out of curiosity.

As it touches the tip of the target, press the clicker and provide a treat. This should also be repeated multiple times per training session and in several sessions per day.

If your fennec doesn't touch the trigger with its nose don't force him or her; just be patient and try again.

Step 4: Once your fennec always touches the target with its nose you are ready to move on to the command stage of the training. Only teach your fennec one command at a time.

Each time your fennec touches the target with its nose, give the command "Target" and then use the clicker and give the reward. Don't repeat the command; be patient. You also need to give a fennec time to carry out the required action. However, if your fennec is a quick and eager learner, fast responses can be reinforced with a really special treat.

Step 5: You now have a fennec that touches the target with its nose and is familiar with the clicker and the "target" command. At this stage you need to present the target but only give the reward *after* and only *if* you have given the command. This way they associate the reward with the command, not the target.

In other words, only give your fennec a treat if you have asked him or her to "target". If your fennec touches the target and you *didn't* give the command, don't give a reward!

Step 6: Several breeders and owners recommend introducing two other commands:

- A "Follow" command. You follow the same steps until your fennec follows the target when you move it or walk with it. This can be used to get your fennec to follow you somewhere such as its cage.

- A "Station" command. Use a brightly colored plastic box or mat as the station. This is used to mark the place or spot where you want your fennec to stay or sit. As with the target, use the clicker and a reward when your fennec touches the station with its nose before moving through the other steps and rewarding your fennec only when it stays at the station.

3) House breaking or toilet training

This is not easy with fennecs. In fact, a number of owners will tell you not to even try to housebreak a fennec. Others will say that you will have partial success with toilet training and that it is worth working for. Partial success is better than none, as it means less cleaning up of urine and feces for you! As with any other training, you will need to be very patient and don't ever punish your fennec; only use reinforcement.

What to use

There are also various options available with regards to where you want to train your fennec to defecate. Some owners say that a cat litter tray works well while others find puppy pads or other large absorbent pads are more effective. The only way to find out is by trying them, as each fennec has different preferences.

It's a good idea, though, to find out what, if anything, the breeder used and continue with the same thing for a while before moving to what and where suits you better.

A litter tray can be best as it more closely mimics their natural behavior: digging in sand. Fennecs are very enthusiastic diggers, so a hooded tray is better so that the litter doesn't get everywhere.

With puppy pads it is much better to get the washable, larger and more absorbent ones because the disposal ones are more likely to be turned into a toy that is dragged around and shredded.

Finally, some owners say you have a greater chance of success if you have more than one litter box or pad and place them in various places in your home and the fennec's enclosure.

How to train

Getting your fennec to use a litter box or puppy pad is not a complicated process (but success is not guaranteed):

- o Let your fennec find the box or pad him- or herself during the course of their normal explorations

- o For the first few days you should take your fennec to the pad or box every hour and place the fox gently in or on it so that it gets used to the smell, feel and where the box/pad is

- o If your fennec defecates somewhere, take it to the box or pad immediately so the connection begins to be made. Do *not* punish your fennec for accidents!

- o When your fennec uses the litter box or pad you must give it a reward so that the desired behavior is reinforced. If you have found a clicker very effective, click and reward each time your fennec defecates where it should.

To further encourage your fennec to use a box or pad they must be kept clean. This also helps with odor.

4) Harness and leash training

This training is most helpful for when you have to take your fennec out, for example for vet visits. It also allows you to take your pet fox for a walk.

But, it's *really* not advisable to take your fennec out until it has learned some basic commands. If it has you may have a small chance of getting your fox back if it escapes.

What to use

It should also be noted that you can't only use an ordinary small dog or a cat collar because an agile, quick fennec can wriggle out of one in no time at all. And, given half a chance, they will.

What you will have to invest in is an H-harness that is the right size for your fennec. These harnesses fit around the body and are therefore much more secure, as they can't slip over the animal's head.

In addition, fennecs don't react well to a harness that must be slipped over the head and those large ears. It should be a design that allows you to fasten the harness over the chest and then the neck.

How to train

Before taking your fennec out, it's also a good idea to get him or her used to the harness. Take small steps and begin by just letting him or her sniff and investigate the harness while you hold it. Don't try and put it on too soon.

Once your fennec is used to being near the harness and is familiar with how it smells and the texture of it, you can start trying to put it on. Proceed slowly and gently and use treats to reward any and all progress made.

If your pet accepts the harness, leave it on for a while when it plays; this helps him or her to feel relaxed in the harness and more used to it. Just remember to take it off so your fox gets used to having it put on and taken off.

However, don't leave your fennec in a collar or harness when it is not supervised in case it gets caught on something, as it could have fatal consequences. Conversely, some fennecs never accept a collar or harness. As with all other training, remember not to get impatient or to force or punish your little fox if it doesn't learn or even co-operate.

Once you have succeeded in training your fennec to wear an H-harness and a lead, and – very importantly – you have practiced for several weeks in a *totally* safe and controlled environment, you can take your fox outside for a walk.

There is a chance that a fennec will not find being outdoors entirely enjoyable, as they may be frightened by perceived threats such as birds of prey, dogs or even airplanes passing overhead.

It's important that you get your fennec used to the leash gradually too. Control him or her gently to start with; don't pull too hard or quickly, as this will scare and even hurt your pet. Both of these will damage your bond and reduce your chances of success with the training. Once your fennec is used to the leash you can increase the amount of control you exert.

5) Training your fennec to sit

The basics are the same as for other types of training: be patient and use treats to reward the right behavior. Other than desirable snacks, no special equipment is needed.

How to train

Bend down, squat or sit on the ground (the idea is to be close to ground level) and hold a treat in your hand. Your fennec will investigate the treat by sniffing it.

Don't give the treat to your fox but rather move your hand and the treat past the fennec's ear and round behind its head. When this is done your pet will follow the movement of the treat with its head and eyes. As it this happens you will find that your fennec sits of its own accord.

When it is sitting give the "Sit" command and the treat. Your pet should, after many repetitions, associate sitting with being given a tasty reward. The next step is to only give the treat if you have given the command and he or she sat as instructed.

6) Final thoughts on training

There are a few guidelines to keep in mind with any training that you undertake with your fennec:

- ✓ Give your fennec time to learn and then follow a command
- ✓ Don't repeat commands and never punish your pet
- ✓ If your fennec seems anxious, restless or distracted, stop the training session and try again later
- ✓ Repeat training exercises on a regular basis or he / she will forget.

Chapter 9: Caring for your Fennec Fox

1) Grooming

As a general rule you won't need to groom your fennec, as they are clean little creatures and self-groom. However, there may be instances when he or she has become very dirty or sticky and a bath can't be avoided. You can use a very mild cat or dog shampoo.

There are two important notes when it comes to bathing your fennec. Firstly, don't run water when it is in or near the bath or basin, as they find it very frightening. Secondly, make sure that your dry him or her very thoroughly to prevent a fungal infection developing. This is especially important if the fennec can't lie in a warm spot to dry off.

2) Shedding

Fennec Foxes, like several other canids or canines, either don't shed at all or have a short annual seasonal shed. This usually takes place during summer when a thicker winter coat is shed as a way to help the fox keep cool in the hotter months.

If your fennec is a shedder, you will find that brushing him or her regularly will help to remove the loose hair and also shorten the shedding period.

3) Safety and taking your fennec for walks

Advice with regards to taking your fennec into the outside world needs to be repeated because you really don't want to lose your fox or have it injured or traumatized.

These guidelines should be adhered to:

- Only take your pet out on its harness and leash once it is used to them.

- Only venture into quiet locations because a fennec will easily be frightened if confronted by a potential predator or something frightening such as crowds, traffic or loud noise. A really panicked fennec will get out of a harness or hurt itself trying to. If it gets loose it will take off and your chances of getting him or her back are very small indeed!

- It's recommended by most breeders and owners that you use an H-harness and a collar that are both attached to the leash in some way. With this arrangement, if your fennec starts trying to get away, it has to get loose from two restraints rather than just one. This will take longer and will therefore give you a little more time to react and pick up your fox before it gets free.

Chapter 10: Feeding your Fennec Fox

1) Feeding in the wild

Fennec Foxes are efficient hunters and small animals, eggs and insects make up 90% of their diet. In the wild, a fennec will eat a range of insects, worms, small reptiles including lizards, bird eggs, birds and small rodents.

Their incredibly sensitive, large ears are their primary weapons; they help fennecs to locate prey, including creatures that are underground or hidden under rocks or in vegetation.

In addition, a fennec's amazing agility allows it to pounce on prey from about 4 feet or 1.2 meters away!

Fennecs are also scavengers but that is mainly for roots and other plant matter that is high in water content.

2) What and how much to feed your Fennec Fox

Pet fennecs are not picky eaters and have very healthy appetites. This means it's up to you to supply the right food in the correct amounts or you will have an unwell or an underfed or fat fox.

Fox owners have different ideas about what constitutes a healthy and balanced diet for a pet fennec. However, the majority agrees on or suggests the following:

✓ Fennecs are carnivores through and through and most of what they eat must therefore be meat. Only about 10% of their diet should consist of plant matter such as fruit and vegetables.

✓ Fennecs should be given ¾ cup of food twice a day. Using the 90% and 10% ratio, the vegetable amount of the daily allowance translates to 2 to 3 rounded teaspoons.

✓ The best meat is raw rabbit and you can buy ground rabbit online. Your butcher can probably assist too. Rabbit is lean, good for fennec's kidneys and contains low levels of retinol (a form of Vitamin A that can cause spinal problems in foxes).

By way of comparison, rabbit contains in the region of 6,200IU/kg of retinol, lizards approximately 4,880IU/kg, pinkies are <10 g - 21,333 IU/kg and chicken comes in at about 35,600IU/kg.

✓ All insects are very low in retinol and therefore good for fennecs. They are one of their favorite foods in any event.

✓ Fennecs must have taurine (an amino acid that plays a vital role in metabolizing fat) in their diet. Cooking meat can destroy much of the taurine content. This is why raw meat is better. Fennecs that are fed cooked meat must be given additional taurine.

✓ The optimal diet is a mixture of rabbit and fresh insects such as cockroaches. Fennecs also love certain large worms like mealworms. Both insects and worms can be cultivated by you rather than buying them.

✓ Insects can be trial and error, as some foxes don't react well to certain insects while others love them. This is true, for instance, of crickets, which cause gastric upsets in some fennecs.

✓ The odd raw egg or piece of fish can make a nice change for your pet fox. Small lizards and pinkie mice (mice that are less than 5 days old) can also feature on the menu from time to time.

✓ Most fennecs love fruit. Berries are the best choice, as they are fairly low in sugar. They can also reduce the pungency of fennec's urine.

✓ If you want to use fox food for your fennec you need to select it with great care. It must contain taurine, be a rabbit-based food and contain less than 10% vegetables.

Regardless of what food you opt for and how you prepare it, it is essential to ensure that your fennec has a balanced and nutritional diet to prevent him or her developing health problems.

Keep in mind that high quality protein diets enhance kidney function. They also strengthen the immune system, allowing your fennec to resist infections far more easily.

3) Taurine

Taurine has been mentioned already but given how crucial it is for fennecs it deserves a sub-section of its own. This essential amino acid is found naturally in certain proteins and must be a part of a fennec's diet.

Without adequate taurine in their diets, foxes and other wild canids suffer a range of health issues including cataracts in young animals, reproductive problems and even potentially life-threatening conditions such as cardiomyopathy.

On a more encouraging note, providing taurine may help to reverse or partially address some of these conditions. It also protects against endotoxins (a toxin that is part of the outer wall of a bacteria and is released when the bacteria ruptures or breaks down). This is important and very useful in and of itself but it also reduces the pungency of the urine.

It is thought that a pet fox should be getting in the region of 250 to 500 milligrams of taurine per kilogram of food per day. Feeder mice, including pinkies, which are an ideal size for fennecs, are a very good source of taurine. However, *don't* use them often, as they are too high in retinol to be healthy!

Uncooked foods high in taurine:

- Beef muscle: 362 mg
- Beef liver: 192 mg
- Beef kidney: 225 mg
- Chicken muscle: 337 mg
- Clams: 2400 mg
- Cod: 314 mg
- Lamb muscle: 473 mg
- Lamb kidney: 239 mg
- Oysters: 698 mg

Cooked foods high in taurine:

- Squid: 766 mg
- Octopus: 871 mg
- Crab meat: 450 mg
- Clams: 889 mg
- Scallops: 1006 mg
- Mussels: 596 mg

If you are concerned that your fennec is not getting enough of this essential amino acid, you can add taurine to his or her diet. Some owners simply empty the powder content of a taurine capsule over their fennec's food and mix it in.

A multi-vitamin and mineral supplement that can also be given to fennecs, such as Vionate, is also recommended.

4) Water and your Fennec Fox

Yes, fennecs can go long periods without water. However, a pet fennec is not necessarily going to get all the hydration it needs from its food the way it would in the wild.

It is therefore necessary to make sure that your fox has constant access to fresh and clean water.

5) What NOT to feed your fennec

There are a large number of things that are really bad for your fennec, just as there are for domestic dogs and cats. These guidelines and rules should help you avoid unhealthy or toxic foodstuffs and keep your fennec healthy and happy.

- Don't use cat food or chicken, as they are far too high in retinol. With long-term use, retinol causes spinal problems.

- Pork should be avoided because of its high fat content.

- Don't feed your fennec rodents too often, as they contain more retinol than is healthy.

- Avoid grains and too many vegetables. You will be able to tell from your fennec's feces if you are giving it too much fiber.

- Fennecs shouldn't eat rice, carrots, grains of various kinds, or corn/maize, as they can't digest them properly and therefore don't derive any nutritional benefit from them. These items can even lead to gastric problems.

- Don't ever give your pet fox grapes or raisins. It seems they cause kidney damage, although it is unclear why this is the case or what it is in grapes and raisins that cause the problem.

- Never buy fox food that is low in protein, high in vegetable content and fat and/or contains grains, cereals or other starches. It's really important to study ingredient labels carefully to make sure.

- Generally speaking, you should not give your fennec any of the foods that are bad for dogs because they are also bad, even toxic, for fennecs:

  - Chocolate
  - Citrus fruit
  - Fruits high in sugar such as bananas and peaches
  - Pasta and other starches
  - Sweets
  - Human food and table scraps
  - Onions and garlic in all forms
  - Alcohol and foods containing alcohol
  - Medicines (for animals and humans)
  - Salt
  - Spicy foods
  - Macadamia nuts or foods that contain them
  - Milk and other dairy products
  - Avocados
  - Food or drink that contains xylitol.

- It's best to avoid giving your fennec bones, especially cooked ones, because they are very brittle and can splinter and cut or pierce the throat or digestive tract.

Of course this does not hold true of the tiny, light bones in reptiles and pinkie mice, which fennecs can deal with.

6) Raising insects and worms to feed to your fennec

There is no need for you to spend money on insects or worms for your fennec. You also don't have to prowl around in your garden or local park or woods to look for food for your fox. The other option is to raise these tasty and nutritious foods in your home.

You will need to get a 'starter pack' from a large pet store or online. Each species should come with instructions about how to care for and feed the critters that will in turn feed your fennec. There are, however, a few guidelines for some of the more popular fennec feasts.

➢ *Meal worms*: These worms should be kept in the cups or tubs they are sold in. Place a few inches of a medium they can feed on such as crushed monkey biscuits or wheat germ.

They will eat various types of ground meal and vegetable matter such as carrots, apples and potatoes. Some feed mealworms small amounts of powdered milk, as it is thought to raise the protein content in the mealworms.

Keep them in the refrigerator to slow down their growth because they grow, mature, and die quickly, so you want to slow down this process rather than loosing most of them.

➢ *Silkworms*: Silkworms can also be fed to your fennec and they are very high in protein.

These sedentary worms need a dry, warm environment; a large- or medium-sized cardboard box works well. Plastic tubs are less successful for housing silkworms because these containers get too warm for them. The optimal container is a "silkworm keeper", which can be bought at a retailer or online.

In terms of their diets, silkworms require specific kinds of leaves such as freshly picked and washed mulberry or beetroot leaves.

➤ *Super worms*: Don't let these critters get too big before you give them to your fennec, as you don't want food that is too large for your fox to eat with safety and enjoyment.

These super-sized and active worms should be housed in a tub or plastic box that prevents them from crawling out. A large plastic box with a screen lid is usually effective. They must have a lot of space and food or they will eat each other!

Super worms need bran or oats and water in the form of carrots or other vegetables.

➤ *Cockroaches*: You need to know what type of cockroach you have, as some are climbers and others aren't. If they are non-climbing roaches, you can use an ordinary tub or a box to keep them in.

However, climbing roaches need special arrangements so they can't get out of the container. One simple way to prevent them getting out is to (a) use a higher container than for the non-climbing roaches and (b) smear some Vaseline below and around the rim of the container so that they won't be able to get on the sides and will slide or drop down into the container.

As many people know, cockroaches will eat anything that qualifies as food and are far from picky!

➤ *Mice and rats*: These rodents are not an option as they multiply very fast, are hard work to keep clean and – most importantly – should not form a regular part of your fennec's diet because of their high retinol content. You will end up with dozens and dozens of rodents that your fennec can't have…

If you want to give your fennec a pinkie now and then, buy them from a pet store.

Chapter 11: Health management

Fennec Foxes are fairly hardy. However, no matter how robust a living creature is, it is not immune to illness and disease and injuries can happen too.

Many of the health issues fennecs are susceptible to are the same ones domestic dogs and other canids fall prey to.

1) Choosing a vet

Some breeders say that you should find a vet that knows about foxes, while others feel you at least need to find a vet that specializes in exotic pets. Nether of these is an option for many fennec owners.

However, you can take comfort from the fact that many fox owners believe that as long as you have a good, trusting relationship with your local vet and he or she is prepared to care for fennecs, that is the best arrangement to have.

Given the similarities with domestic dogs in terms of health issues, many vets are fairly willing to take on fox patients. A good vet will be willing to do research or talk to a colleague who does have solid knowledge of fennecs.

In addition to treating your fennec if it gets sick, your vet will advise you on various routine preventative measures such as vaccinations, flea control and deworming.

2) Vaccinations & other preventative health care

Vaccinations

When you buy a fennec kit from a breeder, find out from him or her which vaccinations your new baby fox has had. Professional and reputable breeders will probably supply you with a vaccination record and medical history. If the initial vaccinations have not been done you need to have them administered as soon as possible.

Many of the vaccinations your young and adult fennec will need are those you would also have administered for pet dogs. They include vaccinating against rabies, distemper, parvovirus and adenovirus. However, be guided by the breeder you buy your fennec from and your vet.

A vet who is familiar with exotic pets and foxes will be able to recommend an effective and safe combination vaccine that will protect a fennec against the range of standard canine illnesses.

It should be noted that *only* killed or recombinant vaccines should be used for foxes, as their little bodies can't fight off live vaccines and what should guard their health may kill them. Furthermore, the minimum dose should be used because of their size.

There is also strong anecdotal evidence that the MLV vaccine that is used to protect dogs from distemper is *not* safe for use in foxes. Fennecs especially, due to their size, have been reported as developing distemper following administration of the MLV vaccine. It is thought that this is because the vaccine is a modified live one and fennecs can't fight off the disease and develop distemper as a result.

In terms of rabies vaccinations, allow yourself to be guided by your vet. There are some areas where the chances that your fennec will be exposed to rabies are negligible, so the vaccine can be avoided.

On the other hand, having your fox vaccinated will put your mind at ease if your fennec nips you or somebody else. In addition, if a person asks a doctor to do a rabies test following a bite, doctors in many states and countries are legally bound to report it. This can have dreadful consequences, especially for your fennec, which may be put down.

Vaccinations are done according to a specific schedule and your veterinary practice will advise you about these in terms of what vaccine is needed when and how often.

Annual vet examinations and check-ups

When you take your baby fennec to the vet for the first time, it is suggested that you have a blood test done in order to determine a healthy baseline. This will give your vet something to compare later blood test results to. Your vet may in fact opt to do two baseline tests initially.

The reason blood tests are so important is that older fennecs are a little prone to liver and kidney problems. If your vet knows your fennec's healthy blood profile he or she will be able to spot these health issues, and heart problems, early and begin treatment without delay. Early treatment can literally be a lifesaver.

Older fennecs should have an annual physical examination and blood test that looks for any signs of kidney or liver problems. Some breeders suggest that middle-aged fennecs (6 years old or more) should have blood tests done twice a year.

Part of any regular examination will include testing fecal matter for evidence of internal parasites that can then be dealt with.

3) Parasite and flea prevention and control

Parasite control

Like all animals, fennecs are also susceptible to internal or intestinal parasites. This is especially true of pets that are fed foods such as rodents that may themselves have parasite infestations.

The good news is that intestinal parasites can be easily controlled by dosing your fox with a parasite control medication once a month. Your vet can recommend a suitable one. These products also provide instructions as to dosage and so forth.

Unfortunately, fennecs are prone to heartworm. These nasty parasites can cause very serious health problems. The good news is that they are easy to prevent. They must be prevented because curing them is anything but easy!

External parasites include organisms such as mites. These may not expose your fennec to serious health risks but they are not pleasant, as they cause itching and, in some cases, allergic reactions.

Secondary issues arise when, due to allergy or excessive scratching, the skin becomes inflamed and painful. In severe cases, the skin is broken and an infection may set in.

Flea control

As with dogs and cats, fleas can cause your fennec a great deal of discomfort and irritation. There are various preparations available on the market. You can use one for cats or small dogs to keep fleas off your fennec.

It's important, though, to use an anti-flea product regularly and to use one that deals with fleas at all the stages of their life cycle. Fleas, the health issues associated with them and flea control is discussed again later in the chapter.

4) Neutering or spaying a Fennec Fox

Having your fennec spayed or neutered when it is young is not mandatory. However, sterilization is strongly recommended by breeders for both behavioral and health reasons.

Behavioral advantages

Having a young male neutered will greatly reduce territorial urine marking, aggression and sexual behavior towards inanimate objects, other animals, etc.

Spayed females may become friendlier and a little more affectionate after being sterilized.

Health advantages

Taking your fennec to the vet for spaying or neutering when they are still young will contribute to a life that is both healthier and longer.

Specific benefits for male foxes are the prevention of prostate enlargement and cancer of the testicles. Neutered males are also less likely to get perianal tumors.

Females have a significant reduction in the risk of diseases of the reproductive system and breast cancer/cancer of the mammary glands.

5) *Common Fennec Fox illnesses and health problems*

Common signs of illness in Fennec Foxes

While one can acquire the knowledge to make a more accurate diagnosis in terms of the health issue your fennec is suffering from, there are some general signs and symptoms all owners should be on the lookout for:

- Loss of, or marked reduction in, appetite
- Weight loss
- Vomiting and/or diarrhea
- Difficulty defecating or urinating
- Blood in the urine or feces
- Coughing
- Growths or lumps
- Listlessness or lethargy
- Weakness or lameness
- Bloating of the abdomen
- Labored or unusual breathing.

If symptoms persist and/or worsen, or you are in doubt about what the problem is, it's better to err on the side of caution and consult your vet.

Common diseases and ailments

a) Heartworm/Dirofilariasis

Heartworms or *Dirofilaria immitis* are a parasitic nematode or roundworm. A mosquito carries the parasite. About seven months after a bite from an infected mosquito, the larvae in the blood mature into adult nematodes.

They move through the circulatory system and eventually lodge in the heart and, to a lesser degree the lungs, and the surrounding blood vessels. Once there, the worms begin to reproduce.

The more worms in the fox's body, and the longer the infestation goes on, the more severe the disease. In addition, some canids are more badly affected than others by this nasty parasite. If the condition is left untreated, the animal will die.

Foxes and domestic dogs are both prone to these roundworms, which are found all over the world, particularly in regions that have tropical or subtropical climates. They are also prevalent in river basins and along certain coasts including the Gulf and Atlantic coasts.

Symptoms

Symptoms vary depending on the severity of the infestation. Foxes are diagnosed with Class I, II or III:

- Class I: This low level of infestation doesn't usually cause any visible symptoms at all. Some animals may develop a mild, infrequent cough.

- Class II: With a more severe case of these nematodes there are usually two symptoms: coughing and an intolerance to exercise. This is especially noticeable in fennecs, as they are usually so active.

- Class III: Animals that have a severe *Dirofilaria immitis* infestation can be very ill indeed. They may be suffering from marked exercise intolerance, shortness of breath, high blood pressure, irregular and very rapid heart beat, anemia and may even faint from time to time. In the worst cases, these parasites cause right-sided, chronic heart failure.

The prognosis for a fennec suffering from mild or moderate infestation is good. However, the outlook for foxes with Class III infestations is not nearly as good or as certain.

Causes

There is only one way your fennec can pick up heartworm: the bite from an infected mosquito that carries the *Dirofilaria immitis* larvae. These mosquitos are also the only way the disease spreads.

The larvae move from the site of the bite through the body via the blood. After approximately six or seven months, these larvae reach the heart and the blood vessels around the heart and lungs. Once there, the larvae settle and begin to mature and grow.

A fully-grown, adult heartworm is very thin but can reach a length of 12 inches or 30.5 centimeters! It's easy to see why and how a tangled mass of heartworms can cause very serious blockages and obstructions in the heart, lungs and blood vessels. Even a single heartworm presents a significant danger.

These parasites then reproduce and release immature heartworms – called microfilariae – into the host's bloodstream. These remain circulating in the blood and if an infected fennec is bitten by a mosquito, the parasite will be passed on in the blood.

Once inside a mosquito, the microfilariae become heartworm larvae, which will in turn be passed on to the next creature that mosquito bites.

Diagnosis

A physical examination is combined with blood tests that look for evidence of the female heartworm antigen, a urine test and even X-rays to look for enlargements or distensions in blood vessels.

In addition, a vet may use an electrocardiograph (ECG) to look for disturbances or abnormalities in the heartbeat or rhythm or the heart itself. For example, with severe infestations, the right ventricle of the heart can become enlarged because of the mass of parasites in it.

Treatment

Treatment must involve killing the parasites. However, the treatment carries risks and therefore has to be controlled carefully.

The fennec will be hospitalized as part of the initial treatment just so the animal can be monitored. A medication called an adulticide is administered, which kills the adult heartworms.

If there have been complications such as blood clots, additional treatment is needed and the sick animal will have a longer hospitalization period so that the complications and parasitic infestation are both dealt with.

For severely affected foxes, surgery is necessary in order to remove the obstruction caused by the adult worm or mass of worms from the heart or a major blood vessel such as the pulmonary artery. This surgery is usually performed via the jugular artery in the animal's neck.

The microfilariae circulating in the blood stream are killed by using a monthly preventative medication. This ensures they don't reach the heart, lungs and major arteries, where they can reach maturity and reproduce.

Managing the condition and further treatment

After a fennec has received treatment for a heartworm infestation, they need further care at home.

For four to six weeks after the administration of the adulticide, the fox must be kept quiet by significantly restricting their movement. Foxes that were very ill should be kept in their cages for this period to ensure they don't rush about in usual fennec fashion.

If a fox suffered from congestive heart failure due to the presence of a worm or worms in a heart ventricle, the vet may also suggest a slight reduction in the sodium content of the foxes' diet.

The vet will run an antigen test four months after the adulticide was administered to check for the presence of adult *Dirofilaria immitis*. If the test is positive, another dose of adulticide will be given. The vet may opt to perform surgery on animals that appear to be resistant to the medication.

However, if a fennec is not showing too many symptoms or it is frail or old, a vet may look at and discuss the possibility of not re-administering the treatment. The primary reason for this option is that the medication can cause lung problems.

Prevention

The best option is – as is so often the case – prevention rather than cure. This is especially true for a parasite that can be so hard to eliminate.

Your vet will recommend the best preventative medication. These prophylactic or preventative treatments are very effective and should be administered to your fennec regularly.

It is essential to administer the necessary medication as regularly as your vet recommends or the manufacturers indicate. Without this your fennec could get sick or re-infested.

b) Neoplasia

Neoplasia is a blanket term used for various types of growths, lumps or masses. There are two main types of neoplasia:

- Benign: these neoplasms don't invade the tissue around them and as a result they don't spread. They are not usually fatal unless they are very large and place marked pressure on a significant blood vessel or an organ.

- Malignant: these are what are more commonly called cancers. These growths move into the healthy tissue around them and destroy it. Parts of these cancerous growths, called metastases, may separate from the main mass and form tumors in other parts of the body.

Fennecs are prone to neoplasms in the mammary glands (around half of the growths in mammary glands are malignant), skin, neck, head, mouth, testicles, prostate, abdomen, urinary tract and the immune system.

While they can occur in fennecs, bone, kidney and lung cancers are fortunately rare. However, they are very dangerous when they do. This is especially true of cancer or carcinoma of the kidneys, which usually affects both kidneys.

Causes

As with abnormal or cancerous cell growth in any species, neoplasms are caused by a disruption of the normal birth and growth of cells. Instead of forming and behaving as they should, the cells become abnormal in both structure and growth.

The exact triggers of cancerous cells in particular are still not fully understood.

Cancer is more common in older fennecs than in young ones.

Symptoms

Symptoms will vary depending on where the growth or cancer is located. However, a general list is as follows:

- Sores that don't heal even with treatment
- Swellings or growths that don't go away and in fact increase in size
- Loss of appetite
- Marked and sustained weight loss
- Inability to eat or swallow
- An unpleasant or sweet odor
- Bleeding or discharge from any orifice (body opening)
- Difficulty breathing
- Vomiting and/or diarrhea (more likely in cases of neoplasms in the digestive system)
- Problems urinating or defecating
- Stiffness or lameness
- Listlessness or fatigue

Seizures are more specifically due to tumors or growths affecting the nervous system. However, significant weight loss and listlessness is common across all cancers in fennecs.

Early detection is particularly important with malignant neoplasms; the earlier treatment begins, the better the prognosis or possible outcome for the affected fox.

Diagnosis

The first stage of an accurate diagnosis is a very thorough physical examination by a veterinarian. Based on what he or she finds, this will be followed by a number of tests.

The tests include urine and blood tests and may well include radiography and imaging studies of various kinds, which could include Ultrasound, X-ray Computed Tomography (CT scan) and

Magnetic Resonance Imaging (MRI). These are all aimed at establishing exactly where the growth is and its size.

Finally, a vet may well perform a biopsy. This involves taking a tiny sample of the abnormal tissue to confirm the diagnosis and/or determine the type of cancer.

Treatment

There is not a one-size-fits-all treatment for cancer. The course of treatment will be entirely determined by the location, size and type of cancer, the fennec's age and its overall state of health.

Prevention

Don't give yourself a hard time with this question. Given the causes of cancer are not established, it's impossible to guard against or prevent it. However, there are a few things you can do to reduce some of the risks:

- ✓ Have your fennec sterilized before he or she is a year old/before they become sexually mature. This will help to prevent mammary gland, testicular and prostate cancers.

- ✓ Don't expose your fennec to environmental toxins such as chemical sprays, certain cleaning agents or cigarette smoke.

- ✓ Take your fennec for regular check-ups at the vet, as someone who knows what to watch for is more likely to catch the cancer early.

c) *Renal/kidney failure*

Kidneys are vital organs, as they perform a number of crucial functions. These include the regulation of water in the blood, blood volume and blood sugar and pH levels. The kidneys also produce red blood cells and certain important hormones. Without these processes and substances a fennec is in a lot of trouble!

The danger with kidney disease is that it can develop very slowly over an extended period of time. A fennec owner may only spot the symptoms too late for effective treatment.

Kidney disease can be treated. However, chronic renal or kidney failure can't be cured. In addition, the damage done to the kidneys can't be reversed. The best outcome is to slow the progress of the condition.

Symptoms

Symptoms may vary from one fox to another and appear gradually. The group of symptoms that are associated with this disease are:

- Diarrhea and/or constipation
- Loss and lack of appetite
- Vomiting
- Weight loss
- Increased thirst
- Blood in the urine (known as hematuria)
- More frequent urination
- Increase in urine quantity
- Lethargy
- Depression
- Seizures
- Sudden onset blindness
- Coma.

Given fennecs don't usually drink much water, the increase in thirst is perhaps easier to notice than it is with dogs and cats.

Causes

There are several possible causes of kidney failure. They include a blockage or obstruction in the urinary tract, diabetes mellitus, genetic factors, some medications, kidney disease and lymphoma (cancer in the lymphatic system).

Diagnosis

An examination by a vet is not enough to diagnose kidney failure. Several tests are also required.

A full range of blood tests including a chemical blood profile and full blood count must be carried out. A blood count looks at the number of red and white blood cells, the oxygen-carrying protein hemoglobin, the number of platelets, and the ratio of red blood cells to the liquid component of blood. In addition, a urinalysis must be done.

Chronic renal failure often gives rise to a number of other health issues including higher than normal blood pressure and anemia. Electrolyte levels will be abnormal and the levels of chemicals such as nitrogen, urea and creatinine in the blood will be elevated. This is also true of protein enzymes.

An examination of the urine shows that, because the kidneys are no longer processing urine as they should, it is not concentrated or diluted.

A vet may also decide on X-rays and ultrasound in order to assess the kidney's size or shape. It is not unusual in cases of chronic renal failure that the kidneys shrink and become abnormally small.

Treatment

The most common treatment for fennecs with chronic renal failure is fluid therapy. This helps to counteract dehydration by replacing the lost bodily fluids.

Changes in diet may also be necessary but are more difficult with fennecs. Ideally a canid with renal failure should be placed on a restricted protein diet. A vet will help plan and manage this so the fennec's overall health is not adversely affected.

Your vet may also prescribe a Vitamin D supplement and a phosphorous binder (these reduce the absorption of phosphate). In combination these improve the balance of phosphorous and calcium in the fennec's system.

Renal failure and its treatment can also lead to stomach problems including ulcers and gastritis (inflammation of the stomach lining). In order to deal with this and boost the fennec's appetite, vets prescribe additional medications.

Blood pressure that is too high or too low also needs to be medicated and foxes that are not producing enough red blood cells require a medication that stimulates cell production.

Managing the condition and chronic care

Kidney failure is incurable and irreversible. However, there are two things you can do. Firstly, you can take steps to slow down the progress of the disease. Secondly, there are changes you can introduce to make your fennec's life more comfortable by reducing the severity of the symptoms.

One such measure is to put your fennec onto a specially-formulated diet. These foods are low in sodium, protein, calcium and phosphorous but high in omega 3 and omega 6 fatty acids and potassium. While these foods are most effective in reducing the symptoms of renal failure there is a downside: they are unappetizing.

Fortunately, you can overcome this lack of flavor fairly easily and your vet will give you some guidance on the matter. Many fennec owners mix a little stock (chicken or beef) or some other flavor enhancer into the food. Just be careful to select one that is low in sodium.

Foxes with kidney failure can become dehydrated. In severe cases, a vet will place him or her onto a drip or administer injections just below the skin. When caring for a fennec at home it is essential that you ensure that there is always plenty of fresh, clean water. This should also be supplemented with foods that contain water.

Finally, because renal failure is a chronic disease, it is essential that your fennec goes to the vet for regular and frequent check-ups.

d) Liver disease

The liver, like the kidney, is an important organ. Its primary functions are the removal of toxins from the system, aiding digestion and playing a role in blood clotting. Without these jobs being performed by the liver, an animal becomes ill.

The good news is that liver disease can be treated or at least managed in the majority of cases.

Symptoms

The symptoms shown by fennecs with liver disease are similar to those for a number of other medical conditions. Broadly speaking they are:

- Loss and lack of appetite
- A distended abdomen due to fluid build-up (called ascites)
- Vomiting
- Diarrhea
- Weight loss
- Blood in the urine (known as hematuria) or the feces
- More frequent urination
- Weakness
- Unsteadiness when walking
- Jaundice (yellowing of the whites of the eyes, gums and tongue)
- Confusion or disorientation
- Seizures.

If untreated, liver disease can lead to hepatic encephalopathy, which is a serious brain condition.

Causes

Liver disease has multiple possible causes. These include:

- Infection
- Trauma/injury to the liver
- Aging
- Medications, for example long-term use of painkillers
- Another disease such as diabetes or problems with the pancreas
- Untreated heartworms
- Diet, for instance too much fatty food
- Genetic factors
- Mold on vegetables
- Some plants and herbs.

Diagnosis

The vet will examine your fennec, ask you about its diet and check medical history in terms of other current or past illnesses and any medications.

Blood tests will be done to look at liver function and blood count. X-rays and ultrasound may also be used. If these tests indicate that it is necessary, a biopsy of the liver may also be performed.

Treatment

There are two factors that dictate the course of treatment: how severe the liver disease is (how bad the damage is) and what the underlying cause is. However, broadly speaking, there are four treatments that are used either on their own or in combination:

o Changes in diet: the vet will either suggest a specialist food or provide a diet plan for your fennec. One of the main features will be a reduction in the amount of fat in the diet while still ensuring adequate calorie and nutrient intake.

o Medication: the nature of medications or combinations used and the duration of administration will be determined by the condition of the fox and the cause of the liver disease.

o Supplements: certain supplements can help the liver tissue to recover. For example, milk thistle is often recommended.

o Surgery: this is only a treatment option if there are cysts or some other type of growth.

The goal of any and all treatments is to reverse the damage or cure the disease and to prevent the condition worsening to the point of liver failure.

Prevention

The good news is there are things you can do to protect your fennec from liver disease.

Firstly, feed your pet a good, balanced diet that is low in fat. Secondly, don't allow him or her to wander around and eat plants or insects that may be toxic and harmful in some way.

e) Heart muscle disease (Dilated Cardiomyopathy)

Dilated Cardiomyopathy (DCM) is a diagnosis that is given when the heart – both the upper and lower chambers – has become enlarged as a result of diseased heart muscle. Often one side of the heart is more affected than the other. The heart no longer functions properly as a result of this enlargement.

When it is enlarged the ventricle, or lower heart chamber, doesn't pump blood properly to the body and, even more problematically, to the lungs. Without adequate blood supply fluid begins to collect in the lungs.

There is often a further complication. Because the heart has to work so much harder than normal it becomes strained and congestive heart failure (CHF) will result.

DCM and CHF are both more common in older fennecs (5 to 10 years) than in young animals.

Symptoms

There may be others but the most common symptoms and most easily observable symptoms are:

- Lethargy/listlessness
- Loss of appetite
- Weight loss
- Rapid breathing
- Coughing
- Panting
- Distended abdomen
- Fainting.

Symptoms that are revealed through a thorough veterinary examination and various tests include:

- Slow or weak pulse
- Abnormal contractions of the heart muscles, which affects the pumping action of the heart
- The blood capillaries fill more slowly than they do in a healthy fennec
- Breathing sounds are dull and muffled

- A crackling sound can be heard in the lungs due to fluid collection.

Causes

The cause of DCM is unclear. Two theories are genetics and taurine deficiency.

Diagnosis

A thorough examination by a vet is necessary. He or she will listen to the heart and lungs and may also do blood tests to rule out other conditions or complications.

Before a firm diagnosis can be made, a vet will run a number of tests including scans or other types of radiographic imaging to look for enlargement of the heart and/or fluid in the lungs.

Specifically, an ultrasound or echocardiograph is used to assess the heart ventricle's ability to contract, the size of the heart generally and the size of the left upper and lower ventricles specifically. An electrocardiogram (ECG) will establish the existence of an irregular and/or abnormally rapid heart beat.

Treatment

The treatment for this condition consists of medications only. The purpose of treatment is twofold: to treat the symptoms of congestive cardiac failure and to improve the functioning of the heart. The types of medications that used are:

- Cardiac medication that improves heart contraction
- Medication that slows down rapid heart beat
- Diuretics to reduce and control the amount of fluid that collects in the lungs
- Vasodilators cause blood vessels to dilate, which makes it easier for the heart to pump blood through them and to pump effectively.

Managing the condition

One needs to be realistic about the prognosis for this condition. Canids including fennecs with DCM will only live for 6 to 24 months after diagnosis. What a loving owner can do, however, is make the remaining time as comfortable and happy as possible.

It is essential to take a fennec suffering from DCM to a vet for regular and frequent check-ups. Your fennec's progress will be measured through the use of blood pressure checks, X-rays, ECGs and blood tests.

In between visits to the vet, a fennec owner must be watchful and look out for symptoms that recur or worsen. It's also important to assess your fennec's mood and general behavior, as these are also good and helpful indicators of his or her health or lack of it.

f) Pneumonia

There are two types of more complicated pneumonia that canids including foxes and domestic dogs are susceptible to.

Pneumonia is an inflammation of the lungs, which causes fluid to collect in the lungs and in the sections of the airways in which carbon dioxide and oxygen are exchanged. This makes breathing difficult and reduces the amount of oxygen in the blood reaching the various organs.

Bacterial pneumonia

As the name implies, bacterial pneumonia is an inflammation of the lungs caused by a bacterial infection. If the condition is quickly and appropriately treated, the prognosis is generally good.

However, there can be complications. This type of pneumonia can give rise to two other serious conditions: sepsis and hypoxemia. Sepsis occurs when toxic, pus-generating bacteria make their way into the blood stream and poison the entire system. Hypoxemia is diagnosed when the levels of oxygen in the blood are severely low.

Symptoms of bacterial pneumonia

- Coughing
- Breathing difficulties including rapid breathing
- Wheezing
- Loss of appetite
- Weight loss

- Fever
- Nasal discharge
- Rapid heart rate
- Lethargy
- Intolerance to exercise.

Not all fennecs with bacterial pneumonia will exhibit the same or all of the symptoms. A vet will also pick up others by listening to the lungs and breathing sounds with a stethoscope.

Causes of bacterial pneumonia

There is no one single bacteria responsible for pneumonia in foxes. However, in canids the two main – but not only – culprits are *Bordetella bronchiseptica* and *Streptococcus zooepidemicus*.

Fennecs that have a viral infection, a weak immune system or a metabolic disorder are more susceptible to bacterial pneumonia than healthier animals.

Diagnosis of bacterial pneumonia

As usual, diagnosis will begin with a thorough physical examination. If this indicates the need for further tests, these will include X-rays of the lungs and chest, blood tests that will show the presence of infection through higher than normal white blood cell counts, a urine test and a throat culture may also be taken to assess which specific bacteria is responsible.

Treatment of bacterial pneumonia

If the bacterium is not known, a broad antimicrobial or antibiotic medication will be prescribed. If a culture was done to identify the bacteria, then a more targeted or bacteria-specific medication is used.

The other symptoms will also be treated if they are severe or the fennec is very ill. For example, hospitalization may be necessary and medications aimed at reducing fever, easing the bronchial spasm in the lungs and improving appetite may be administered. If the fox is dehydrated, a drip will be set up to replace fluids and electrolytes intravenously. In the case of marked breathing difficulty, oxygen will also be provided.

Managing bacterial pneumonia

When your fennec is well enough to come home or if you are treating it at home, you need to pay attention to several things.

Firstly, you need to try to keep your fennec relaxed. While it is feeling unwell it won't be too hard. Once he or she is starting to feel better you need to restrict its activities and movement. In addition, while any sick creature needs rest to heal, a pet with pneumonia shouldn't be allowed to lie in one position for too long because this allows fluid to collect in a single area.

Secondly, your vet will prescribe a medication or several, which must be administered regularly and in accordance with the vet's instructions. He or she may also recommend physiotherapy for a fox with badly congested lungs.

Next, you will need to make any changes to your fennec's diet that the vet directs. Often this diet will be high in protein and aimed at giving your fox the nutrients and energy it needs to fight the infection and get strong again.

Finally, take your fennec back to the vet for check-ups so that progress can be monitored and assessed. Initially, these vet visits may well involve an examination, blood test and chest X-rays.

Prevention of bacterial pneumonia

The only steps you can take are to maintain the overall health of your fennec by feeding it the correct diet, monitoring its well being and health, and having it vaccinated regularly against preventable infections.

Aspiration pneumonia

Aspiration pneumonia is the result of particles of regurgitated food or gastric acid getting into the lungs and causing inflammation.

Gastric acid is very corrosive and damages the lung tissue. The particles of food often also set up an infection in addition to causing inflammation.

Symptoms of aspiration pneumonia

The symptoms are very similar to those that occur with bacterial pneumonia:

- Coughing
- Breathing difficulties including rapid breathing
- Wheezing
- Loss of appetite
- Weight loss
- Fever
- Nasal discharge
- Lethargy
- Intolerance to exercise
- Rapid heart rate
- A bluish tinge to the gums and skin (cyanosis).

Causes of aspiration pneumonia

This condition may develop after vomiting or as the result of a separate medical condition such as a neuromuscular illness, a problem with the esophagus or an abnormality of the pharynx or the esophagus. In some way and to different degrees all of these conditions cause difficulties with swallowing.

Diagnosis of aspiration pneumonia

Because bacterial and aspiration pneumonia are so similar in terms of symptoms, a vet needs to take particular care with a diagnosis so that both the underlying cause and the pneumonia can be suitably dealt with.

The vet will begin with a thorough physical examination, which will include listening to the lungs and heart and assessing the presence and degree of fluid in the lungs.

Other tests including X-rays of the chest and lungs, a complete blood count and a chemical blood profile will be carried out. The X-rays will show the presence of aspirated matter in the lungs and the blood tests will look for evidence of an infection.

In the event that a fennec is having marked difficulty breathing, the vet may also elect to have a blood gas analysis done. This shows the levels of oxygen and carbon dioxide in the blood. That in turn gives an indication of how well or poorly the lungs are functioning.

If infection is found, additional tests will be done to identify the bacteria involved. Knowing which bacterium it is makes it possible to use a targeted antibiotic.

In order to rule out and/or deal with an underlying problem, vets may also administer a swallow test to make sure that there are no problems with the muscles in the esophagus or with the pharynx. If there are, a further investigation is needed to correct the issue or the fennec is likely to get aspiration pneumonia again.

Treatment of aspiration pneumonia

This nasty form of pneumonia is a life-threatening condition. In light of this, a fennec is likely to be admitted to the veterinary practice for several days to stabilize its condition and kept in intensive care conditions.

If the aspiration pneumonia is due to a condition affecting the fox's ability to swallow, the overall prognosis for him or her is unfortunately not good.

If the aspiration happened recently, suction is used to remove the foreign matter from the lungs. Oxygen will be given to any fox that is having great difficulty breathing, as this helps to stabilize its condition.

Aspiration pneumonia can result in shock and this must also be treated. The degree of shock will determine what the treatment will involve.

In addition, a fox that has had pneumonia for a while is likely to be dehydrated because of the loss of appetite, stomach upsets and fever. This, too, must be treated. However, given that swallowing may be a problem, fluids should be administered intravenously and not orally.

Managing the condition and home care

A fennec recovering from aspiration pneumonia needs rest in a place where it will not be disturbed. Keeping it quiet in its cage or enclosure initially is best.

When it is a little stronger, some exercise is important because it results in some coughing, which in turn helps to clear the lungs.

The owner needs to be vigilant and monitor their pet's condition. As with bacterial pneumonia it's important not to let your fox lie in the same position for too long, as fluid will collect in one area and cause further problems.

The vet will certainly prescribe medication, which you must administer regularly in accordance with directions. Physiotherapy will also help to clear badly congested lungs.

A vet may also suggest changes in diet. For a fennec with no problems with swallowing, a diet high in protein provides the nutrients and energy it needs to get strong again.

Lastly, regular check-ups must be done. This allows the vet to monitor and assess progress. These visits will involve a physical examination, blood test and chest X-rays.

g) Atopic Dermatitis

Atopic dermatitis is a chronic condition. It is an inflammation of the skin that is caused by an allergic reaction. Just as people can be allergic to common substances such as grass, dust or mold, so can animals including fennecs.

Your fennec's allergy may not be apparent immediately and allergies usually develop when the fox is between three and six months old. In addition, even when the allergy is present, the symptoms may be so mild at first that they aren't noticed.

Symptoms

The symptoms of atopic dermatitis may get worse at certain times of the year depending on which environmental allergen is causing the problem. Symptoms may also get worse over time.

Symptoms of this condition are itching leading to excessive licking, scratching and rubbing against objects, flaky dry skin or greasy skin that has an unpleasant odor, hair loss and chewing or nibbling at the affected areas.

If the scratching, licking, rubbing and nibbling go on for too long they can lead to inflamed and raw, red-looking areas on the skin, which can become infected. Sores also form and they can be very slow to heal because of the ongoing scratching etcetera. As the condition worsens, so does the pain and general discomfort experienced by the fennec.

The parts of the fennec's body that are most likely to be affected by atopic dermatitis include:

- Between the toes
- On the pads of the paws
- Stomach
- Underarms
- Groin area
- Wrists
- Ankles
- Ears
- Around the eyes
- Muzzle.

Causes

Common allergens include pollens from trees, grasses and even weeds, spores from mold and mildew, house dust mites and even the dander from other animals. The term dander refers to microscopic pieces of dead skin and/or hairs that become airborne and settle on surfaces including skin and hair.

Diagnosis

As with all medical conditions, the first step will be a thorough physical examination. In an effort to identify the allergen, the vet will ask for a medical history and information about the fox's environment.

Some vets do blood tests to look for allergy-related antibodies in the blood. However, these tests are not always reliable or conclusive.

Intradermal or skin tests may also be performed. This test involves injecting very small amounts of allergens into the skin. If a rash or inflamed bump results, this helps to pinpoint the allergen responsible for the dermatitis.

Treatment

The vet will decide on a course of action depending on what is causing the allergic reaction or dermatitis.

If your fennec is hyposensitive to allergens, then specific and long-term therapy can be given recommended. Over the course of 6 to 12 months the vet administers injections of the allergen that is causing the problem. As the fox becomes used to the substance, the allergic reaction diminishes. However, this approach is not successful in all cases.

A second option is medications that help with the itching. The two classes of medications used to treat atopic dermatitis are antihistamines and corticosteroids. Some of these are not tablets but sprays that give relief from the itch and inflammation.

It should be noted that many of these medications and sprays ease symptoms; they do not treat or cure the underlying condition.

Managing the condition

The fact of the matter is that atopic dermatitis will sometimes go through phases when it eases or goes into remission. Ever more rare are the odd cases where the condition vanishes of its own accord.

Something that can help ease the itching and discomfort are cool baths and using a shampoo that is very gentle and has anti-itch properties. Your fennec will let you know if the baths help or are just a source of stress or distress.

As with any other medical problem, you need to administer a medication that is prescribed and take your fennec to the vet at the intervals he or she feels is necessary based on your pet's condition. Usually the frequency of vet visits decreases after the first couple of months or when the symptoms appear to be under control.

Prevention

Prevention will be also dictated by the nature of the allergen. If it's a substance that can be remove from the fennec's environment the problem will resolve itself. Unfortunately that is not always easy.

In any event, your vet will offer advice and guidance about how to minimize exposure to the allergen responsible.

h) Flea infestation

Fleas are parasitic insects that jump onto hosts and then bite them in order to feed off the host's blood. They live in the hair or fur of the host, where they cause discomfort or worse.

Most pet owners are unfortunately all too familiar with fleas and the problems they cause. Dogs, cats and fennecs all pick up fleas from other animals or from the environment.

The bite from a flea causes itching. Unfortunately a pet will seldom have a single flea! A fennec with fleas can become very itchy and distressed. Complications arise if a pet develops or has an allergy to fleabites, specifically to flea saliva.

In the case of allergies or fleabite-induced atopic dermatitis, the itching is far worse than usual and it can be accompanied by skin inflammation, hair loss and possible sores and infection.

Symptoms

The most obvious symptom is increased, sometimes almost frantic, scratching. In severe cases the skin becomes inflamed, raw or infected and there may be a degree of hair loss.

Diagnosis

Working out that your fennec has fleas is not difficult. You don't need a vet to handle this diagnosis unless your fennec has had an extreme or severe reaction.

Unlike mites, fleas are visible to the naked eye, as they are roughly the size of a pinhead. These little copper-colored insects walk on the surface of the skin and prefer to stick to places where there is less light such as the armpit, groin and tummy regions.

In addition, fleas leave what is commonly and euphemistically known as "flea dirt". These very small black grains are flea feces: the digested and excreted blood from the host.

If you are not sure if what you are finding on your fennec and on his or her bedding is in fact flea dirt, there is a simply test you can carry out. Place one of the grains on a damp piece of paper towel or toilet paper. If it is dried blood/flea dirt it will start to make red streaks on the paper after a couple of minutes.

Treating fleas on your fennec

For your fennec's sake and yours you need to deal with fleas as quickly and effectively as possible.

You want to provide your pet with relief from the irritation and itching and you also need to prevent the fleas from spreading to other pets or infesting rugs, carpets and other soft furnishing. Fleas are not above feasting on people's blood either!

There is no instant fix for these parasites but there are a number of effective products on the market that address the problem. Some are tablets taken orally, there are shampoos too and other remedies are powders or liquids that are applied topically. Other fennec owners opt for flea collars but these do pose hazards such as strangulation if the collar gets hooked on something.

What is very important is to select a product that kills fleas at each stage of the life cycle. If not, you will never successfully eradicate them.

The life cycle of the flea

There are various anti-flea products available but to select the best one you need to look at which stage of the life cycle the product targets.

Fleas begin as eggs, move to the larval stage, then the pupa or cocoon phase before finally becoming adults. The pace at which the parasite moves from one stage to the next depends on host availability, temperature and other environmental factors. However, the usual period from egg to adult is approximately 14 days.

An adult female flea usually lives on her host for several weeks. During this time she will feed by sucking blood from her host two to three times daily. Even more disturbing is the fact that she will also lay up to thirty eggs on her host each day! Some eggs will remain in the host's fur or hair while others will drop off and land on bedding, floors, carpets and so forth.

Regardless of where they are, the eggs will hatch and the tiny worm-like larva will emerge. They will feed on whatever they can find: adult flea feces, dead skin cells on a host and even plant matter.

As the larvae grow they molt twice and then form a cocoon that contains a pupa. The cocoon can survive a long time until the environmental conditions are suitable. Within its hard casing the pupa is protected and will only emerge when it senses vibrations, carbon dioxide and heat as these all indicate the presence of a host nearby. A just-hatched flea jumps onto the detected host and the cycle begins again.

Treating fleas in the environment

In order to effectively deal with fleas you need to treat all your pets, including ones that don't show signs of having fleas… yet. In addition, pet's bedding must be washed in soapy, hot water.

All rugs and carpeting must at least be vacuumed although steam cleaning is preferable. If your vacuum cleaner model uses bags, throw the bag away.

The final step is the use of some kind of chemical treatment such as a multi-ingredient aerosol fogger that kills fleas at every stage in their life cycle. Another product is a sodium borate based powder that is applied to carpeting and flooring.

If you are dealing with a severe infestation in your home and/or your fennec's enclosure it might be a good idea to get in a professional pest control company.

If you'd rather avoid chemicals and follow a more natural route you can obtain non-toxic nematodes from an online or retail pet shop. These are then introduced into the areas where there are fleas. These nematodes will eat the flea larvae. While this is more eco-friendly it does not address each stage of the life cycle.

Your vet or the breeder you bought your fennec from is the best person to get advice from on flea control and prevention.

Flea-borne diseases

Fleas cause itching and bites can lead to inflamed, raw or infected skin and even hair loss. All of these are very unpleasant for your fennec but fleas can pass on far more serious, even fatal, illnesses.

- Allergic/atopic dermatitis: This condition is discussed in detail in g) of this chapter. Fleabites are one cause of this nasty reaction, which may lead to more serious conditions as a result of complications.

- Tape worms: These are segmented flatworms that can grow to 28 inches or 71 centimeters. Some fleas carry tapeworm eggs, which they have picked up from a host that had the parasite. If your fennec swallows a flea carrying eggs they will hatch in its stomach.

  The young tapeworm passes into the intestine where it attaches itself to the wall. A tapeworm infestation causes vomiting, weight loss and itching around the anal area. It's unpleasant but is certainly not life threatening and many canids live for years with tapeworms.

- Haemobartonellosis: Although canids are more likely to pick up this disease from ticks, it can also be transmitted by fleas. Haemobartonellosis affects the red blood cells. While some animals are only mildly affected, others develop anemia, weight loss and dangerously elevated heart rates. A severe case that is not treated can be fatal.

- Plague: This is a bacterial infection carried by some fleas. A pet with this illness will develop a severe fever and its lymph nodes become very swollen. The real danger with this virulent infection is that it develops very fast and it can kill very quickly too. It is also very infectious so other pets must be kept away from an infected fennec.

i) Ticks

Ticks, like fleas, are blood sucking insect parasites. There are some species that are found all over the world and others that are specific to certain continents. They are more prevalent in some areas than others and more of a problem in the spring and summer months than during colder times of the year.

Removing a tick that has gorged itself on your fennec's blood is not a pleasant experience. It's also not easy to remove some ticks. If they are not removed at all or completely they don't just cause irritation to your pet. They pose dangers to your fennec, as they carry serious diseases.

Diagnosis

It is easy to spot ticks on your fennec. You will also feel them when you cuddle, pet or groom your pet. Ticks engorged with blood are especially hard to miss, as they become large and bloated.

Different tick species are different sizes and colors. They are often found in areas where the blood supply is close to the surface such as on and in the ears and elsewhere on the head and neck.

Treating and preventing ticks on your fennec

Ideally you want to keep ticks away or prevent them rather than dealing with them once they have latched on to your fennec. Fortunately, there are a number of preventative methods that are available.

- Shampoos: There are shampoos that are readily available from your vet or a pet store, which kill ticks on contact.

However, in light of the fact that many fennecs don't enjoy water, this may not be the best option. The second disadvantage is that a shampoo treatment lasts much less time than other remedies. You may have to bath and shampoo your fennec twice a month during tick season, which is not ideal for either of you.

- Powders: These treatments are formulated to kill ticks that are already on the animal and also to repel others so that they don't attach themselves. It must be applied both to the pet and its bedding. While some of these powders are effective, they have drawbacks.

  Firstly, they need to be applied weekly during tick season. In addition, they are labor intensive as they must be massaged into the hair so that it reaches the skin. Finally, these are very fine powders and the dust from them can cause problems if they are inhaled or go into your fennec's eyes: the skin, eyes and mouth can become irritated and even inflamed.

- Oral medications: Medications in pill form offer a number of advantages for you and your fennec. These preparations will deal with ticks and also break the flea life cycle so you can kill two parasites with one dose.

  They are also only administered monthly and with ease as they can be hidden in food or some kind of tasty snack.

- Dips: These are also probably not the best option for a pet fennec, as he or she will not enjoy having their hair wet through with a chemical solution, even if it is diluted.

  Getting the mixture right is also critical so that your fennec's skin is not burnt or badly affected and it does not ingest unhealthy amounts when it grooms its fur.

- Sprays: This product is also effective and acts fast. It both kills ticks and coats the hair, repelling other ticks. The down side is that it causes severe irritation if sprayed near the eyes and mouth. Furthermore, your fennec may find the sound frightening.

- Collars: These keep ticks off the neck and head but are not useful as the only way of killing and repelling ticks or protecting the rest of the fox's body. In addition, the collar should come into contact with the skin and that's easier said than done when the fur is as thick as it is on a fennec. Collars can also set off an allergic reaction or skin inflammation and may pose a danger if they get hooked on something.

Treating ticks in the environment

Removing ticks from your pet fennec and keeping them away is one part of the war against these nasty parasites. You also need to treat the environment in which your fox lives. There are a number of things you can do:

- If you have a severe tick infestation, consider calling in a professional exterminator.

- In less serious cases, and as a preventative measure, you can use one of the granular, spray or powdered products that are sprinkled or sprayed on the ground, bedding and other areas your pet uses. These are available from pet stores, online, vets and even some garden centers.

   It is crucial, though, to ensure you use a product that will not be harmful or toxic if ingested or on contact. Your vet or a fennec breeder can advise you on the most suitable and safest products.

- It is also a good idea to keep the grass on your property mowed and shrubs trimmed or pruned so that ticks (and fleas) have fewer hiding places.

Monitoring your fennec for ticks

It's very important to regularly check your fennec for ticks. This is especially crucial if your pet is housed outdoors or goes for walks where there is long grass or overgrown greenery. In fact, it may be a good idea to simply not to take your pet fox for walks outside of your property during tick season.

Areas of your fennec that you should check with particular care, as they are popular with ticks are the groin, the armpits, between the toes, around the pads of the paws, inside or around the ears and deep in the thick fur on the neck. All of these locations are where the tick can be well hidden and where the blood supply is close to the surface or easy to access.

If a tick has attached itself and is engorged with blood you need to take great care to remove it immediately and completely; no part of the tick's head or body should remain. Ticks that are still moving around in the fur must also be removed but that is easier to do.

Tick-borne diseases

There are a large number of different ticks. While some carry the same diseases, others are specific to one species of tick. What's more, certain tick species carry more than one disease.

The illnesses they carry are serious and if they cause more than one medical condition the risks to your fennec's health are very great. The other bad news is that tick-borne diseases can be hard to spot. There are several common diseases that affect both canids and, often, humans.

- Lyme disease: This infection attacks both canids and people and leads to lameness. In worst-case scenarios or severe cases this illness is fatal. Diagnosis is difficult as many of the symptoms mimic other illnesses.

  Symptoms may be slow to emerge and can come and go. Fennecs and other canids don't develop a rash at the bite site the way people do. The primary symptoms are short-term lameness that lasts several days, fatigue and lethargy and loss of appetite.

- Anaplasmosis: This disease is carried by the same species of ticks that carry Lyme disease. Canids bitten by these ticks may therefore contract both diseases. There are two forms of Anaplasmosis: *Anaplasma phagocytophilumis* and *Anaplasma platys*.

  - *Anaplasma phagocytophilumis* is an infection that targets the white blood cells and weakens the immune system and the ability to fight infection. Humans can also contract this nasty infection. The symptoms include lameness, lethargy, neck pain and loss of appetite.

- *Anaplasma platys* affects blood platelets, which leads to problems with clotting/bleeding disorders. The primary symptoms are nosebleeds, bleeding gums and bruises on the body and in the mouth.

- Hepatozoonosis: Unusually this disease is not contracted from a tick bite. Canids get this illness when they swallow an infected tick. This disease also has two different forms:

  - *Hepatozoon americanum* causes a seriously debilitating condition as it attacks the muscle cells. In severe cases this disease is fatal. Symptoms include chronic weight loss, loss of muscle mass, general pain, fever, depression and discharge from the eyes.

  - The symptoms of *Hepatozoon canisis* include appetite and weight loss and lethargy.

- Babesiosis: This disease is unusual in that it is transmitted through a tick bite and the bite of a canid that has been infected. It can be contracted by people and animals.

  As a result of the disease's effect on the red blood cells the immune system attacks the infected blood cells. The result of this is a number of symptoms: overall weakness, loss of appetite, vomiting, weight loss, anemia, fatigue and marked lethargy.

- Tick paralysis: This is not so much a disease as a very severe reaction to the toxin that ticks secrete. This toxin attacks the central nervous system and symptoms first appear about a week after the animal was bitten.

  Canids, including fennecs, become very weak and they often develop a limp as a result of the effects of the toxin. The signs may be apparent in the rear legs first but then affect all four limbs. More severe symptoms are difficulty swallowing and then with breathing. Death usually follows.

The good news is that recovery is, in most cases, both very rapid and complete if the tick is found and removed early on. If symptoms have progressed they will need to be treated. For example, a fox that is struggling to breathe will need oxygen and to be treated with an antitoxin.

j) Conjunctivitis

Conjunctivitis is an infection or an inflammation of the conjunctiva, which is the moist tissue that lines the inside of the eyelid and covers the eyeball itself. The condition is more common in animals that have allergies, suffer from dry eyes or from some sort of autoimmune disease.

Symptoms

The symptoms of this painful eye condition are hard to miss:

- Redness
- Swelling underneath the conjunctiva due to a collection of fluid
- Clear or opaque discharge from the eye. A yellowish or white discharge often indicates the presence of pus
- Frequent blinking
- Squinting
- The eyeball looks 'cobbled' due to the formation of lymphoid tissue containing white blood cells.

Causes

Conjunctivitis as a primary condition (rather than when it is a secondary issue caused by something like dry eye or allergies) has several causes.

- Bacterial infections of the eye and sinuses
- Viral infections
- Immune system related included allergies
- Cancer tumors
- Benign or non-cancerous lesions

-   Inflammation of the cornea or sclera (the white of the eye)

This condition can also be due to or caused by other medical conditions that affect parts of the eye. These include glaucoma (abnormal pressure in the eyeball), diseases of the eyelid or the eyelashes, ingrown eyelashes or non-functioning, blocked or absent tear ducts.

Conjunctivitis can also be a complication following an injury to the eye or because of the presence of some sort of foreign body including dust. Both of these leave the eye vulnerable to infection and often cause marked inflammation.

Diagnosis

Even if the symptoms seem straightforward, the fact that there are so many potential causes means that it is essential for a vet to examine a fennec that has sore, runny and/or red eyes.

The vet will need to diagnose the problem by screening for all the potential causes of conjunctivitis. In other words, he or she will look for any other eye conditions by carrying out a very thorough examination.

➤   The eye, eyelids and eyelashes will be looked at to see if there is any foreign matter caught in or on them that might be causing the problem

➤   A fluorescein stain is spread on the surface of the eye. This will show any foreign objects, lesions, scratches, ulcers or other injuries to the conjunctiva or eyeball

➤   Eyeball pressure will be measured to rule out glaucoma

➤   If there is any evidence that there may be an infection of the sinuses that has spread to the eyes, the sinus cavities will be irrigated or flushed out

➤   A skin test may also be performed if allergy-related conjunctivitis is suspected in order to identify the allergen responsible

➤   If there is evidence of growths on the eye the vet may perform a biopsy to establish the nature of the growth

➤ In the case of discharge from the eye, a sample will be taken and a culture done in order to establish which bacteria or virus is responsible.

Treatment

Because there is such a wide range of possible causes, treatment will be determined by what has given rise to the condition. However, cleaning or flushing the eye with a sterile fluid to remove any matter including discharge is often a first step.

A bacterial infection will be treated with antibiotics. A viral infection won't respond to antibiotics but the symptoms can be managed while the infection runs its course.

If an allergy is the culprit, changes will need to be made to the fennec's diet or environment, depending on the nature of the allergy. Once the allergen is removed the conjunctivitis should clear up. Symptomatic relief is given in this situation too.

Some conditions require surgery of varying severity to correct them: tumors and ingrown eyelashes must be removed and blocked tear ducts must be opened and cleared. Surgery for cancer may be followed by secondary treatment such as radiation.

In cases where the disease or illness is very severe, the eyeball will be removed. It is sometimes necessary to remove the surrounding tissue as well.

Your vet may also put your pet fox in a collar, sometimes called an Elizabethan collar, so that he or she can't scratch or paw at its eyes. If it does scratch or rub, the condition may worsen or the recovery process may be slowed down.

Managing the condition

As with treatment, what you need to do to care for your fennec will depend on why it developed conjunctivitis.

If your vet provides a new diet plan, it must be adhered to no matter how much your pet begs for the now forbidden foods. If the allergen is not a food but something in the environment, you will need to take all the steps you can to eliminate the allergen. This is not always easy with air-borne ones especially.

If your fennec's conjunctivitis is viral or bacterial you need to keep him or her away from your other pets, as this condition is highly infectious.

Whatever medications, solutions or ointments the vet prescribes must be administered in accordance with application and dosage instructions. It's very useful to have someone who can help you, as putting drops or cream in a wriggling fennec's eyes on your own is almost impossible!

Finally, remember to take your little fox for check-ups as often as the vet suggests. However, if his or her eyes seem to be getting worse, or if it appears that the treatment doesn't seem to be helping, don't wait for the scheduled appointment; visit the vet immediately.

k) Ulcerative keratitis or corneal ulcers/erosions

The cornea is the transparent layer at the front of the eye. It has two very important functions. In addition to allowing light to enter the inner eye, the cornea protects the iris and the pupil. If the deep layers of the cornea become damaged and lost for some reason, an ulcer forms in the cornea.

Depending on where it forms, a corneal ulcer or ulcerative keratitis is classified differently. If the ulcer is closer to the surface of the cornea it is described as superficial while an ulcer towards the back of the cornea is referred to as deep.

Symptoms

What is confusing is that many of the symptoms of corneal ulcers are similar to those of conjunctivitis. For this reason a vet should examine your fennec so that the diagnosis is accurate.

Ulcerative keratitis is a painful condition and some of the symptoms are behavioral. Symptoms include:

- The affected eye waters a great deal
- The eye looks red

- The animal paws at its eye because it is painful
- Squinting
- There is discharge from the affected eye
- The eye is very sensitive to light
- The eye may be kept closed.

A symptom that is more specific to this condition, however, is an opaque film over the eye.

Causes

The causes of corneal ulcers are numerous and include infection (either viral or bacterial), injury or some other trauma to the eye such as a scratch during a fight, or a foreign body in the eye. Ulcerative keratitis can also be a complication arising from another medical condition.

Fennecs that can't produce enough tears to keep the eyeball moist, lubricated and clean are at risk of ulcers. This is also true of foxes that are unable to close their eyelids completely or suffer some degree of paralysis in a facial muscle.

Chemical burns are a further cause, as are ingrowing eyelashes, which can irritate the cornea and lead eventually to an ulcer.

Diagnosis

An accurate diagnosis will involve a very thorough examination of the eye and cornea by a vet. He or she will in all probability use dyes in drop form, as they show up the ulcers on the cornea.

Some vets will also take samples of the discharge or liquid on the eye in order to do cultures for bacteria and fungi. This will help to eliminate conjunctivitis as a possible diagnosis. Blood tests may be done to look for the presence of a viral infection.

Treatment

As with other medical conditions with several possible underlying, causes the treatment for corneal ulcers varies.

With deep ulcers or lesions that are increasing in size and/or depth, surgery may be necessary. After surgery, a collar will be used to prevent the fennec from pawing at or scratching their eye. Activity must also be restricted during the recovery period.

More superficial ulcers will be treated conservatively. The vet will use a swab to gently remove the affected tissue from the surface of the cornea. Another alternative to surgery is the use of a contact lens, which covers and protects the eye from further irritation from the eyelid.

In the case of infection and in order to avoid infection following surgery, antibiotics – usually in ointment form – are prescribed. These are often accompanied by drops to lubricate the eye and stimulate tear production, if that is necessary.

Pain and inflammation will also be addressed through the use of painkillers and nonsteroidal anti-inflammatory medications.

Superficial ulcers should heal fully in approximately a week. Deeper or more severe ulcerative keratitis heals more slowly and will take about two weeks after surgery.

Managing the condition

Your fennec must be kept relaxed and movement should be limited while they are healing and still being treated. Keeping your pet in its cage or enclosure during this time is recommended.

All prescribed medications, solutions or ointments must be administered in accordance with the instructions. If your fennec is in a collar, leave it in place until the vet says it can be removed.

Take your pet for check-ups with the vet. However, if his or her eye seems to be getting worse or not healing, don't wait for the scheduled appointment and take him or her to the vet immediately.

l) Glaucoma

Glaucoma is a condition that affects one or more, usually both, eyes. With this condition there is pressure on the eye and, as a result, there is inadequate fluid drainage.

If untreated, glaucoma causes chronic pressure on the optic nerve behind the eye. The result is blindness. Unfortunately, it is not an easy condition to treat in canids.

Types and symptoms of glaucoma

Primary glaucoma is a sudden onset condition where the eye is not draining properly. The symptoms are:

- Blinking
- Red or bloodshot white of the eye
- The front of the eye appears opaque or cloudy
- Dilated pupil regardless of light conditions
- High pressure in the eyeball
- Eyeball looks sunken
- Poor vision.

With long-term or untreated glaucoma that has become severe, the eye begins to degenerate and vision is lost as a result. In addition, the eyeball may become very enlarged and protuberant.

Secondary glaucoma is usually the result of an eye infection. It is also the more common of the two types. Although several of the symptoms are the same as the symptoms of primary glaucoma, there are also significant differences between the two:

- Red or bloodshot white of the eye
- The front of the eye appears opaque or cloudy
- Constricted pupil regardless of light conditions may occur
- High pressure in the eyeball
- Debris within the eye caused by the inflammation
- The iris may stick to the lens
- The iris may adhere to the cornea
- Headaches may be experienced
- Loss of appetite and resultant weight loss
- Lethargy.

You will know your fennec's head hurts because he or she will press it against surfaces to try and ease the sense of pressure or ask for more head rubs than usual.

Causes

There are several possible reasons why the pressure in the eye increases, leading to glaucoma.

Underlying eye conditions that prevent the normal drainage of fluid from the eye are one of the culprits. The most common is the abnormal development of the filtration angles within the eye.

Other causes of glaucoma that are common in canids – both fennecs and domestic dogs – are lens luxation or slipping, injury to the eyeball, tumors on or in the eye or severe inflammation of the eye.

Diagnosis

The vet will take a detailed medical history from you: when the problem began, what symptoms you noticed and whether there may have been an injury.

The examination of the eye itself involves the use of a tonometer, which measures the eyeball or intraocular pressure. Often if the glaucoma happened very suddenly or your vet has other concerns your fennec will be referred to a veterinary ophthalmologist for further tests and a more specific diagnosis in terms of cause.

The veterinary ophthalmologist will look for abnormalities in the filtration angles by carrying out a test that measures the anterior or back of the eye. This test is called a gonioscopy. X-rays and ultrasound are also helpful in terms of finding abnormalities in the eye. Finally, the ophthalmologist will assess the level of vision loss and how likely it is that sight will be regained or if the poor vision or blindness is permanent.

Treatment

The primary goal of all treatment options for glaucoma is to reduce the pressure in the eye as quickly as possible to prevent blindness and alleviate the great pain the condition causes. This lowering of pressure is usually achieved through a cocktail of medications.

A further treatment option is to drain some of the fluid from the eye and use cold to kill the fluid-producing cells in the eye. This process (cyclocryotherapy) slows down or may even stop the glaucoma from getting any worse because no more fluid is being produced within the eye.

Serious cases of glaucoma, regardless of the type or cause, may require emergency surgery in an effort to relieve pressure and protect the optic nerve from further damage.

In animals that have suffered from the condition for an extended period and where the optic nerve has been damaged beyond repair as a result, the affected eye is removed surgically. If both eyes have to be removed your vet will advise you on how to help your fennec adjust to the total loss of sight. Most canids adjust remarkably well.

Managing the condition

Taking care of a fennec with glaucoma involves two aspects. The first is caring for the affected eye if the condition has been diagnosed early enough. This involves the correct and regular administering of medications and making sure your pet visits the vet for eye pressure tests and other monitoring.

Secondly, you and the vet need to monitor the good or unaffected eye too. Statistically the majority of canids will develop glaucoma in the 'good' eye within 8 months. Whatever preventative care can be given should be provided along with treatment of the eye that has already been affected.

Prevention

Primary glaucoma can't be prevented. However, the risk of secondary glaucoma can be reduced – but not eliminated – by guarding against the conditions that may give rise to it.

m) Histoplasmosis

Histoplasmosis is an internal infection caused by the fungus (*Histoplasma capsulatum*), which is found in soil and in the droppings of certain birds and bats.

This fungus, once it is inhaled or ingested, causes severe problems with the gastric and/or respiratory system.

Symptoms

The symptoms that occur most commonly in infected animals are lethargy, poor or loss of appetite, weight loss and diarrhea (this is accompanied by straining while defecating).

Other symptoms that may be present include:

- High fever
- Weakness and lethargy
- Lameness
- Coughing
- Difficulty breathing
- The lymph nodes become swollen
- The appearance of the eyes and skin change
- Enlarged liver
- Jaundice (yellowing of the gums, whites of the eyes and other tissue)
- Enlarged spleen
- Pale gums
- Mucous membranes become very moist.

Causes

Transmission of the fungus is through bird droppings (including chickens and other poultry) or soil that is contaminated with this fungus and its spores.

If a fennec eats or inhales matter that contains this fungus it enters the digestive tract or the lungs. Fennecs, for example, may become contaminated when they dig in soil. Once in the body, the fungus grows and causes disease to develop.

Diagnosis

The vet will begin with a thorough physical examination. This will be followed by several tests to make a firm diagnosis of histoplasmosis: a full blood count, chemical blood profile and urinalysis.

The first complication with diagnosing this condition stems from the fact that some of the tests will confirm that an animal has been exposed to *Histoplasma capsulatum* but not that the disease it is suffering from is a result of this exposure. For instance, tests may show that your fennec has histoplasmosis anti-bodies but that is not the same as having the condition.

The second complication is that many of the symptoms are common to several other conditions. For instance, weight loss, lethargy and diarrhea are indications of a myriad of other medical problems. As a result, further tests will be necessary in order to ensure the correct diagnosis is made and that other conditions are ruled out.

Treatment

The most frequent treatment program involves medication that the owner administers at home.

Canids with histoplasmosis don't usually require hospitalization. The exceptions are firstly if they are struggling to breathe or, secondly, if their digestive system is so compromised they can't absorb nutrients as usual.

Both of these situations can lead to further complications or death. In these cases the fennec will be placed on oxygen or they will be hydrated and fed via tubes until they are stronger.

Managing the condition

This is a very debilitating condition so it is very important to limit your fennec's activity initially. Cage rest is recommended until he or she is recovered.

You need to monitor your pet too in case there is a relapse.

Prevention

To prevent your fennec picking up this nasty disease you need to protect him or her from exposure to the fungus that is responsible for it.

In order to achieve this, don't allow your fennec to dig around in soil where poultry or birds leave droppings. If there are bats in the vicinity you need to make sure your fennec doesn't go near them either, as the soil below and around where they roost will also be contaminated.

n) Distemper

Distemper affects the canid family (foxes, wolves and dogs) and several other wild species. It is a viral disease that is extremely contagious and also, unfortunately, incurable.

Animals that are suffering from respiratory or gastric infections are more susceptible to the disease. In addition, young and non-immunized animals are far more at risk than others. Given fennecs don't react well to distemper vaccines they are among the high-risk group.

Causes

Distemper belongs to the *Morbillivirus* class of viruses and the family *Paramyxoviridae*. Some of the other members include *Rinderpest*, which infects cattle, and *Rubeola* (measles), which attacks humans. All are highly contagious viral infections.

Animals contract the virus when they come into contact with the saliva, urine or blood of an infected animal. The virus can be airborne when a carrier sneezes and it will be present on the food and water bowls and the bedding of pets with distemper. In very rare cases pets have developed the diseases when they have been given a vaccine that was too potent.

Symptoms and types

Distemper initially infects the tonsils and lymph nodes. Once there, it undergoes an incubation period that lasts approximately seven days, during which the virus replicates or multiplies. The virus then spreads to the gastrointestinal, respiratory, nervous and urogenital systems.

The symptoms of this progressive disease include:

- High fever
- Vomiting
- Diarrhea
- Coughing
- Weakness and lethargy
- Loss of appetite
- Severe weight loss

- Red eyes
- Discharge from the nose and eyes
- Enlargement or thickening of the pads of the feet
- Seizures
- Paralysis.

Pneumonia may also develop as a complication of distemper. As the central nervous system is attacked, lesions may form on the brain. As a result, the animal may undergo changes in its personality with some becoming irritable and even aggressive.

Death may follow in as little as two to five weeks after infection.

Diagnosis

A diagnosis requires running several tests to examine the blood, urine and various tissues.

Distemper usually results in low white blood cell counts. Blood, urine and skin tissue tests will also show whether or not there are antibodies and antigens present. If an animal has been vaccinated then that may explain the antibodies. If it hasn't then the antibodies are evidence of the presence of the disease.

If there are complications such as pneumonia or brain lesions these will be diagnosed by means of a chest X-ray and a computed tomography (CT) or magnetic resonance imaging (MRI) scan respectively.

Treatment

There have been cases of dogs spontaneously recovering from the disease. However, given there is no cure for distemper, the treatment focuses on easing the symptoms and keeping the animal as comfortable as possible.

Treatment will be given to animals that become dehydrated or malnourished and antibiotics are used to treat secondary bacterial infections. Medications will be prescribed to control other symptoms such as seizures.

Managing the condition

You and your vet will have to monitor your fennec so that any complications, infections or worsening symptoms can be dealt with immediately. There should also be regular check-ups at the vet, where tests will be done to assess the progress of the disease.

Medications must be given in accordance with directions and an infected fennec should not share bowls or bedding with other pets. In fact, your vet may advise you to quarantine your fennec or keep it away from other pets so they are not infected.

Survival will depend on how strong the animal's immune system is and on which specific strain of the virus it has contracted.

Prevention

Prevention is difficult with fennecs. With domestic dogs you can have them vaccinated. As stated previously, there is anecdotal evidence that the MLV vaccine is *not* safe for use in foxes, especially fennecs because they are so small.

6) Zoonotic diseases

This is a group of diseases that can be caused by fungi, bacteria, viruses or parasites. What distinguishes them from other diseases is that they are zoonotic: they can be transmitted from animals to humans or humans to animals. In other words, they pose a risk to your fennec, you and your family.

a) Tuberculosis

Tuberculosis (more commonly known as TB) is a highly infectious and serious bacterial infection that is found in human beings, canids (dogs and foxes), cattle and domestic cats.

Canids and people will infect each other if the correct precautions are not taken. In the majority of cases, however, the person has the infection first and passes it on to their fox, dog or cat.

While TB usually attacks the lungs or respiratory system, it can also affect the intestines.

Causes

The two bacteria that are responsible for most cases of TB are *Mycobacterium tuberculosis* (the bacteria found in humans) and *Mycobacterium bovis* (the TB bacteria found in cows). Both bacteria can infect canids.

If the bacteria are inhaled, then the lungs will be affected. If the bacteria are ingested in infected meat or diary products then the digestive system will be attacked by the disease. Inhalation is a far more common mode of transmission.

If your pet is diagnosed with TB you must have all the animals and people who came into contact with it tested for the bacteria.

Symptoms

The symptoms of TB can be confused with those of other conditions. The most common symptoms include:

- Coughing
- Breathing difficulty
- Vomiting
- Diarrhea
- Loss of appetite
- Weight loss
- Increased thirst
- Increased urination
- Jaundice (yellowing of the gums, whites of the eyes and other tissue)
- Dehydration.

The grouping of symptoms may differ depending on how long the animal has had the infection and whether the respiratory system or intestine is affected by it.

Diagnosis

Unfortunately TB is difficult to diagnose. Because of this a battery of tests is required:

- ➤ A full blood count assesses the levels of white blood cells, which in turn indicate the extent of the infection

- A biochemical profile gives an indication of the levels of electrolytes and how well or otherwise the organs are functioning

- Samples of fluids are taken in order to do cultures to identify the specific bacteria

- X-rays are used to examine the chest cavity and lungs in cases where breathing has been affected. However, an X-ray is not enough on its own, as TB looks similar to both cancer and pneumonia in an X-ray

- There are unfortunately only two ways to make a definitive TB diagnosis: biopsy and autopsy.

  - A biopsy involves taking a minute tissue sample from the affected organ or organs. The serious complication is that often these animals are really ill and very weak. As a result, an anesthetic and an invasive procedure could be too much for them and could be fatal.

  - An autopsy is performed after an animal dies so it is too late to treat the condition. Naturally every loving pet owner hopes to avoid that.

Treatment

The treatment situation with TB in canids is bleak.

The reason for this is that it is a highly infectious disease people can catch! As a result most foxes (and domestic dogs and cats) are euthanized if they have TB.

In a few cases medication is used. Unfortunately, success rates are low and the medications are toxic too.

Prevention

While there is a lot of bad news about TB, the good news is it is still very rare in fennecs.

It is essential, though, to take your pet to the vet if you think it might have TB or if it has been exposed to another animal or a person that is ill with the disease.

b) Rabies

Rabies is a very serious infection. Like TB, humans can also contract the illness from an infected animal. Transmission is via the blood or the saliva of an infected animal.

The rabies virus attacks the brain, specifically the grey matter, and the central nervous system. It enters the body through a bite from an infected animal. In some cases transmission can be from a scratch. The virus replicates itself in muscle tissue and then spreads from those cells to nearby nerve fibers. The virus attacks motor, sensory and periphery nerves before moving to the central nervous system in the fluid that is found within nerve cells.

This entire process takes approximately 30 days and an infected animal is unlikely to show many symptoms during this phase. However, once they do begin, the disease progresses very fast.

Symptoms and forms

There are two forms of rabies: furious and paralytic. As the virus works its way through the body and central nervous system of an infected fox, the symptoms change.

The early stage usually lasts about three days and the evidence of central nervous system abnormality is mild. After this initial period the fox will enter the furious phase, or the paralytic phase or a combination of both. In rare cases animals die without showing and significant symptoms at all.

- ➢ Furious rabies is characterized by very marked changes in behavior. This will include increased and marked aggression and "attack behavior".

- ➢ Paralytic or "dumb" rabies is quite the opposite. The infected animal loses co-ordination and becomes very weak. As the disease progresses, paralysis sets in.

The general symptoms of rabies are:

- High fever
- Changes in vocalizations

- Pica (eating items that are not food)
- Hydrophobia (an intense fear of water)
- Hyper-salivation (excessive salivation); the saliva is frothy
- Poor co-ordination
- Changes in behavior, specifically becoming markedly more timid or more aggressive
- Irritability
- Extreme excitability
- Dropped lower jaw
- Paralysis of the jaw and throat
- Inability to swallow
- Seizures
- Paralysis.

Once they immerge, the symptoms of rabies are dramatic and very distressing.

If this communicable and zoonotic disease is not treated very quickly the prognosis is not good at all because the infection progresses extremely rapidly and the central nervous system is so disastrously affected. This in turn leads to vital activities and functions shutting down.

Causes

Rabies is caused by a single-stranded DNA virus (genus *Lyssavirus*, family *Rhabdoviridae*) and not by bacteria. The primary method of transmission is a bite from an infected animal, as the virus is carried in the saliva of the sick animal.

In theory, any mammal can carry rabies. In terms of domestic animals, dogs are one of the most common sources or reservoirs of rabies, with cats less frequently infected. Common wild carriers are foxes, coyotes, raccoons, mongooses, jackals, bats and skunks. Rodents including squirrels are very rarely carriers.

Diagnosis

The nature of the symptoms your fennec is showing will determine the action you should take. A canid with ferocious rabies that is aggressive, for example, must be caged and taken to your vet immediately. If you can't do this because your fennec is trying to bite, contact the authorities, which will send animal control personnel to you. Don't put yourself or a family in harm's way, as a bite or a scratch could infect you too!

A vet will immediately quarantine an animal with suspected rabies. You need to provide proof of vaccinations if you can, as this determines the length of the containment period.

Usually the quarantine and containment period will last ten days if the animal has had a rabies vaccine. In the event the animal is not vaccinated, the quarantine period could last as long as six months. The length can be prescribed by local or regional health and safety legislation.

Other illnesses can cause aggression and a vet will rule these out first. Some vets will run blood tests to look for the presence of the virus. Usually, however, the sick animal will be very closely monitored.

A firm diagnosis can only be made after death by doing an antibody test from fluid samples. The relevant authorities must be informed of all cases of rabies in order to ensure that the disease is contained and no public health risk exists.

Treatment

A fennec that has been vaccinated against rabies and is showing symptoms will die 7 to 10 days after first showing signs of the disease. The disease will progress a great deal faster in an animal that has not been vaccinated.

There is no real treatment once symptoms have developed and rabies is fatal. What care is given is usually supportive and aimed at keeping the animal as comfortable as possible, trying to prevent dehydration and so on. Viruses must run their course, as they don't respond to specific medications the way bacteria do to antibiotics.

If an animal shows progressive symptoms of the disease it will be euthanized. This is by far the most merciful course of action.

Warnings

Avoid coming into contact with the saliva of an animal with suspected or confirmed rabies, as it contains very large amounts of the virus. Rabies is a dreadful disease and leads to a horrible death. Very few animals and people worldwide have survived rabies once they have developed symptoms!

If your fennec contracts rabies and you are aware of any animal that may have been bitten or scratched by your pet you *must* inform its owner.

Similarly, if you are aware of any person who was or might have been bitten or scratched you *must* advise him or her to go for testing and treatment!

You also need to disinfect any area that may have been contaminated very thoroughly. This is especially the case with things and surfaces that have had, or may have had, saliva on them. Your vet or the health authorities can advise you on the best disinfectant product to use.

Prevention

The best defense against rabies is regular vaccines, which offer protection from the virus if your fennec is bitten by an infected animal. In some countries and regions these vaccines are legally required. The breeder you bought your fennec from or your vet will be able to inform you about schedules, vaccines, etc.

The second line of defense is to protect your fennec from wild animals or from dogs that may be infected. This is a further reason why allowing your fennec to wander or taking it on walks to more remote areas is not a good idea.

If your fennec is exposed to a rabid animal you must take it to the vet immediately. You need to exercise caution, as the virus will be on your fennec's skin and you must avoid contact with it; wear gloves or wrap your pet in a blanket.

A fox that has been bitten or scratched but is up to date with its rabies vaccines will be given a rabies booster shot immediately. There will also be a lengthy observation period. The duration varies in different areas and countries in accordance with local legislation.

c) Leishmaniasis

Leishmaniasis is caused by a parasite that affects the skin or the organs in the abdomen or both. This visceral form, which is far more serious, is also called black fever.

The skin reaction is more common in canids, including foxes, and in the vast majority of cases of black fever the skin is also affected. The skin infestation causes hair loss and lesions or sores.

In addition to the skin, this parasite may also affect the eyes, joints and various abdominal organs. These include the liver, kidneys and spleen. One of the most dramatic and severe effects of this condition is the tendency to hemorrhage.

Leishmaniasis is zoonotic and can therefore be transmitted to humans. People usually pick it up from the protozoans that are living in the skin lesions.

This parasite is found in South America, Central America, in the states Ohio and Oklahoma in the US, southern Mexico, Portugal, Spain, the Mediterranean basin, and there have been a few cases in Switzerland, Netherlands and the north of France.

Causes

Leishmaniasis is caused by the parasite *Leishmania,* which is a protozoan (a single-celled organism capable of mobility).

These microscopic parasites are transmitted onto the host's skin by sand flies. The second way a fennec might contract this disease is through a blood transfusion from an animal that is infected.

The host will not exhibit any symptoms during the incubation period, which lasts anywhere from a month or two to several years depending on environmental conditions.

In canids – foxes and domestic dogs – most internal organs are eventually infected. The usual cause of death is renal or kidney failure or systemic disease (one that affects a number of organs or the entire body).

Symptoms and types

The two broad types of leishmaniasis are cutaneous (affects the skin) or visceral (affects the organs in the abdominal cavity). Each type is associated with different symptoms

The symptoms of cutaneous leishmaniasis are:

- Alopecia: the hair becomes brittle and dry and falls out
- Nodules develop on the skin
- Ulcers and lesions form on the skin
- Hyperkeratosis: the skin becomes thick, pale and scaly and the skin on the pads on the paws and around the muzzle become chapped
- Nails may become abnormally long and very brittle.

The symptoms of visceral leishmaniasis are:

- Loss of appetite
- Vomiting
- Diarrhea
- Severe and rapid weight loss
- Nose bleeds
- Inability to exercise; lethargy.

There are also a number of general symptoms that are common with this condition:

- Severe weight loss/emaciation
- Fever
- Diseased lymph nodes accompanied in most cases by skin lesions
- Joint pain
- Bone loss/loss of bone density and strength
- Neuralgia (a nerve disorder that causes pain)
- Muscle pain and inflammation
- Symptoms of renal failure: excessive thirst and urination
- Internal organs such as the spleen may become enlarged.

Not all fennecs suffering from leishmaniasis will exhibit all of the symptoms, regardless of which type of infection they have.

Diagnosis

The first step is a thorough physical examination and taking a medical history. As with some other conditions, your vet will begin by eliminating the possibility of other diseases, which have similar symptoms.

The standard tests will be run: a full blood count, urinalysis and a chemical blood profile. With animals that are very ill, tissue samples or biopsies will also be taken from the skin, bone marrow and the spleen and/or lymph nodes. Fluids may also be sent for culturing. Tick borne diseases and various cancers need to be ruled out as possibilities.

Treatment

For severely ill animals that are emaciated and suffering from chronic leishmaniasis, euthanasia is the most humane course of action.

If your fennec is not seriously ill, treatment is provided on an outpatient basis. One aspect of treatment is a change in diet such as an increase in protein to counter the kidney problems. Your vet will also prescribe medications that will both ease the symptoms of the condition and deal with the parasites.

A vet will usually design a treatment program and diet for each patient depending on the nature, type and extent of the infection.

Warnings

This is also a zoonotic condition. In other words, you and your family can pick up this infection when handling an infected pet. The parasite lives in skin lesions on the host and moves to a new host's skin on contact.

Managing the condition

The other challenge with leishmaniasis is that it can never be eliminated entirely. The condition will become dormant for a while but it will flare up again and require treatment.

You need to monitor your fennec and your vet will also need to keep an eye on things regularly. Your fennec may require some blood tests and the occasional biopsy as part of managing the condition.

Unfortunately, most canids will have a relapse a few months (or a year at best) after the initial diagnosis and treatment. Many vets therefore suggest you bring your pet in for a check-up every two months after the first treatment.

7) A Fox First Aid Kit

While one can't prepare for every eventuality, it is a good idea to keep a first aid kit on hand so you can treat your Fennec Fox immediately if the need arises.

The basic kit should contain the following items:

- A muzzle or a gauze bandage that could be used to muzzle your fennec
- Disposable gloves (2 pairs)
- Gauze squares (various sizes)
- First aid tape
- Rolls of gauze bandage
- Scissors
- Tweezers
- Cotton swabs
- Cotton wool balls
- Small torch
- Magnifying glass
- An eye dropper
- Various size syringes
- Nail clippers
- Nail fail (metal)
- A clean towel
- Rectal thermometer (size suitable for cats or small dogs)
- Lubricant
- Needle-nose pliers
- A bitter-tasting, pet-safe compound to prevent licking
- A towel or blanket to wrap your fennec in or carry it on
- Heat and cold packs.

It's a good idea to also have a few medications in the kit. It is essential, though, to be guided by a fennec breeder or your vet as to which ones will be safe for your pet. Basics could include:

- Pet-safe wound disinfectant
- Antibiotic ointment for external use
- Antibiotic eye ointment or drops
- Eye wash solution/sterile saline solution
- Antidiarrheal medication
- A pet-safe antihistamine
- A cream or spray containing cortisone to treat skin irritations and severe itching
- Activated charcoal. Please note this should not be administered unless your vet has given the go-ahead!

Finally, collect all the important emergency and other contact numbers. In an emergency one is not always thinking clearly, so having the numbers you need to hand can save precious time. Have a card or list that includes your vet's number (including an after hours or emergency number), the pet poison helpline and any other local resources that would be useful.

Chapter 12: Fennec Fox reproduction

Those fortunate enough to have Fennec Foxes, and have both a male and a female, may well be tempted to breed them. The advice from breeders and owners is: "Don't!" And there are several reasons why you shouldn't breed fennecs at home.

1) Breeding Fennec Foxes

There are a number of reasons why trying to breed fennecs is not a good idea. Many of these are behavioral but there are some that are biological. The behavioral problems you may well experience are:

> ➢ Males will become very aggressive and more prone to mark their territory with urine.

> ➢ Females are easily disturbed and distressed when in heat, pregnant and after giving birth. They are more likely to feel stressed in captivity and there is a very strong possibility that she will eat her young as a result.

> ➢ To prevent the babies being cannibalized, you would have to take them away from their mother. This is not handled well by the female fennec and she may become aggressive; your bond with your pet will be destroyed.

> ➢ Bottle-feeding baby fennecs is difficult, as they tend to eat far too fast and may well aspirate as a result. This can cause choking or aspiration pneumonia, which is likely to be fatal in such a young fox.

The bottom line is breeding fennecs is not easy and it is also very stressful for the fennecs are the owner; it is simply not a good idea, especially for beginners.

2) Reproduction

Fennecs reach sexual maturity when they are between 9 and 11 months old. These little foxes are monogamous and live with their mate and their offspring in family units or communities of about ten individuals. Fennecs stay with their mate for life and together the breeding pair defends their territory.

Mating season in the wild takes place during January and February and babies are born in March and April after the gestation period of approximately 50 days. In captivity, mating and births can occur year round and the gestation period may be longer.

Females are on heat for two days. Each fennec pair will usually mate only once a year with the mating process, called the copulation tie, lasting almost three hours. If the first litter is lost and the environmental conditions including food supply are right they will mate a second time two to three months after the first mating. Fennecs may only give birth to a single baby or kit. However, litters may contain up to five kits.

While the mother is pregnant and later when she cares for the newborns, the father brings food and aggressively defends the burrow. He continues to do this until four weeks after the babies are born. He is not allowed access to the kits, though, until they are five to six weeks old. The young are weaned completely when they are 60 to 70 days old.

The kits are especially vulnerable for the first two weeks of their lives. After birth, their eyes are tightly closed and the ears folded. The ears lift and the eyes open when the young are about ten days old. They are not able to fully care for themselves until they are six months old.

Chapter 13: Costs & where to buy a fennec

1) Costs

A further reason why you need to be absolutely sure you want a Fennec Fox is the cost. These little canids are expensive; so is taking care of them.

You will pay in the region of $ 2,000 – 3,000 or £ 1,500 – 2,260 for a fennec. Other once-off costs include:

- Closed litter box: $38 – 64 or £29 – 48
- Harness: $20 – 35 or £15 – 26
- Leash: $15 – 30 or £11 – 22
- Pet carrier: $30 – 100 or £22 – 75
- A suitable cage: $250 or £190
- Building an outdoor enclosure: from $100 or £75
- Bedding: $40 – 100 or £30 – 75
- Food and water bowls: $5 – 15 or £3.75 – 11 each
- Toys: $2 - 10 or £1.50 – 7.50 each
- Training clicker: $2 – 20 or £1.50 – 15.

Ongoing expenses are estimated to be: 400 - 640

- Food: $20 or £15 per week
- Cat litter: $20 or £15 per month
- Puppy pads: $40 or £30 per month
- Flea & tick treatments: $400 – 640 or £300 – 482 per annum
- Annual vaccinations and routine check-ups: $200 or £150

There are expenses that one can predict to a degree. But there are others such as vet bills in the event of illness or injury that can't be foreseen. Similarly, you may also incur greater expense if you construct a larger and more elaborate enclosure. Alternatively, your fennec may not use puppy pads or toys and that means a saving for you.

Note: prices above can fluctuate due to currency conversions,

2) Tips on buying a Fennec Fox

If at all possible, purchase one from a licensed breeder. In America, a fox that has been acquired from a non-licensed breeder may be confiscated. Ask a vet that includes foxes or exotic pets in his or her practice for recommendations about reputable breeders. Furthermore, do research on the Internet. Joining Fennec Fox groups, clubs and forums online is a wonderful way to find information.

Avoid buying a fennec that needs to be rehomed. You can often tell that this is the case because the purchase price will be significantly lower than the usual market price. Rehomed foxes are not a good idea, as the majority of older fennecs won't bond with a new owner. As a result they are far more likely to be skittish, shy or even aggressive.

Chapter 14: Conclusion

1) Do's… in no particular order

- ✓ Learn about Fennec Foxes

- ✓ Make sure you can legally own one in your area

- ✓ Take the time and the trouble to bond with your young fennec and socialize it

- ✓ Maintain socialization

- ✓ Start training early on

- ✓ Ensure your pet receives all the necessary vaccines at the right times

- ✓ Take your fennec for regular check-ups

- ✓ Have your per spayed or neutered

- ✓ Dose your fox regularly to keep ticks and fleas away

- ✓ Make sure you get a cage that is large enough for adult fox and that allows for bedding, décor and movement

- ✓ Ensure that your fennec can't escape from its cage or enclosure

- ✓ Monitor you pet fox carefully for signs of ill health

- ✓ Take the time to set up the cage and enclosure carefully so your lively pet will have space and comfort

- ✓ Feed your Fennec Fox a good diet that is high in taurine

- ✓ Keep a First Aid Kit and contact list handy

- ✓ Ensure its cage, bedding and enclosure are kept clean

✓ Keep an eye on your fennec so you don't accidentally stand on it

✓ Expect mess, noise and chaos.

2) Don'ts… in no particular order

- Forget that this is not a domesticated or tame animal

- Overfeed your little fox

- Feed your fennec a diet too high in retinol

- Leave small items lying around that are a choking or health hazard

- Shout at or punish your fennec

- Include too much vegetable matter in its diet

- Neglect vaccinations and check-ups

- Ignore signs of ill health

- Take it for walks in areas where it may get startled and bolt or come into contact with wild animals

- Leave your fennec unsupervised.

3) And in closing…

This guide's primary purpose is to make sure that you have the information that you need to decide, first and foremost, if this is *really* the right pet for you, for your spouse, for your child or for your household.

If the answer is a confident and honest "Yes", this pet owner's guide will also give you the details that will help you to keep your Fennec Fox healthy and happy.

All animals in captivity should at least live to their usual or expected life span. In fact, given they are safe from their natural predators and receive a good diet and veterinary care they should exceed the average life span for their species.

If you are one of those individuals who commits to owning and caring for one of these amazing foxes you will be rewarded by having a pet that is fascinating, unpredictable, intelligent, fun and beautiful… but be ready for anything as they are athletic balls of energy.

Enjoy your Fennec Fox and teach others about them!

www.ingramcontent.com/pod-product-compliance
Lightning Source LLC
Chambersburg PA
CBHW060116050426
42448CB00010B/1896